Rebuilding Fiscal Democracy

Paolo Liberati • Massimo Paradiso

Rebuilding Fiscal Democracy

How to Bring the Social Contract Back Into Economics

palgrave
macmillan

Paolo Liberati
Department of Economics
University Roma Tre
Rome, Italy

Massimo Paradiso
Department of Economics and Finance
University of Bari
Bari, Italy

ISBN 978-3-032-04858-5 ISBN 978-3-032-04859-2 (eBook)
https://doi.org/10.1007/978-3-032-04859-2

This Palgrave Macmillan imprint is published by the registered company Springer Nature Switzerland AG
The registered company address is: Gewerbestrasse 11, 6330 Cham, Switzerland

Acknowledgments

We would like to thank Professor Peter Sloman, of the Department of Politics and International Studies (POLIS) at the University of Cambridge, for his insightful comments on an earlier version of this book. This book represents an expression of gratitude by the authors to those who, about three decades ago, brought attention to fiscal democracy and to the Italian tradition of *Scienza delle Finanze*: to Professor Pedone, who still inspires us, and to the memory of Professor Sergio Steve. Much of the book was written while Paolo Liberati was a Visiting By-Fellow at Churchill College and a Visiting Scholar at the Faculty of Economics, Cambridge. Special gratitude is extended to Professor David Newbery for making the visiting period possible, and for the opportunity and support provided during the stay at Cambridge. At Palgrave Macmillan, we wish to thank two anonymous referees for their comments and especially Wyndham Hacket Pain, who has been an encouraging and supportive editor.

Contents

CHAPTER 1

Introduction

Abstract This book examines the enduring yet increasingly obscured relationship between taxation and public expenditure within democratic societies, framing it as a foundational element of the social contract. It challenges the contemporary political and economic narrative that equates taxation with wasteful public spending, instead reaffirming its role as a structural mechanism for fostering distributive justice within a cooperative democracy. Drawing on the contractarian tradition from Rousseau to Rawls, the book situates taxation within the broader institutional framework necessary for a fiscal democracy, grounded in the principles of mutuality and reciprocity. It proposes the Democratic Welfare State as a pragmatic approximation of Rawls's property-owning democracy, designed to restore the fiscal contract and counteract market capture of democratic institutions. The proposed model includes restoring comprehensive income taxation, reasserting the taxation–spending link, integrating the benefit principle into fiscal policy, supporting universal access to welfare programmes, and reconsidering the international dimensions of fiscal justice.

Keywords Fiscal contract • Distributive justice • Oligarchy • John Rawls • Democratic Welfare State

P. Liberati, M. Paradiso, *Rebuilding Fiscal Democracy*,
https://doi.org/10.1057/978-3-032-04859-2_1

The purpose of this book is to gather the threads—neglected and even scattered, yet still vital—of the relationship between taxation and public expenditures in a democratic society. This involves not only restoring a connection that has been systematically severed by contemporary political discourse and action, in which taxation is equated with the waste of resources through public spending, but also reaffirming the significance of this link as essential to the very existence of the social contract, and to the realization of the system of rights and duties on which social cooperation in a democracy is founded.

The contractarian view of society—an inherently complex political, social, economic, and moral undertaking—has historically been shaped by idealistic conceptions and political projects, from Rousseau to Rawls, and from the American Constitution to the post–World War II constitutional charters in Europe. This view seeks to reconcile the ideals of liberalism with those of democracy: two traditions rooted in individualistic conceptions of society, yet characterized by differing and often conflicting understandings of the interests that individuals are meant to protect. On the one hand, liberalism asserts individual freedom in both spiritual and economic domains, often in opposition to state interference. On the other hand, democracy requires that the relationships between individuals and society be the result of a collective agreement aimed at realizing a contractualist conception of distributive justice.

In delineating the contours of a just society in his works from 1971 to 2001,[1] Rawls invokes the principles of reciprocity and cooperation among equals for mutual advantage. Each citizen, in this framework, accepts the principles of distributive justice on the condition that all others do the same. Distributive justice thus becomes institutionally embedded and articulated in the design of basic institutions[2]—such as the political constitution, the legally recognized forms of property, and the structure of the economy—which are committed to reciprocity in the allocation of rights and duties, as well as benefits and burdens that make cooperation possible.

To achieve this, Rawls articulates two principles of justice that apply to the basic structure of society. The first guarantees each person equal access

[1] From the first edition of the 'Theory of a Justice' in 1971 to a 'Restatement' in 2001 (Rawls, 1999, 2001).

[2] Rawls (1999, 6–7).

to the most extensive scheme of basic liberties compatible with similar liberties for others. The second—encompassing the difference principle—holds that social and economic inequalities must be attached to positions open to all under conditions of fair equality of opportunity and must benefit the least advantaged members of society. Notably, while the difference principle concerns the distribution of wealth and income, it is only one component of Rawls's broader theory of distributive justice. To ensure the fair value of political liberties and equality of opportunity, each citizen must be guaranteed access to health care, education, and other resources necessary to exercise their basic rights and liberties.

Rawls's vision of a democratic society does not align with the notion of a minimal state. Instead, it requires what he terms a property-owning democracy, in which land and capital are privately held, but concentrations of wealth and income are either dissolved or significantly curbed, without the need to move to a socialist economic system. Such a conception of democracy represents the ideal endpoint of a society committed to eliminating political and economic inequalities and preventing the formation of oligarchic power. As Rawls—invoking Rousseau as much as himself—observes: "[A] reason for controlling political and economic inequalities is to prevent a part of society from dominating the rest. When those two inequalities are large, they tend to go hand in hand. [This] allows the few, in virtue of their control over the political process, to enact a system of law and property ensuring their dominant position, not only in politics, but throughout the economy. This enables them to decide what gets produced, to control working conditions and the terms of employment offered, [...] all of which in good part determines what society becomes over time".[3]

In contrast to Rousseau's republic—where the purpose of the social contract is to secure freedom by eliminating inequality through taxation and public spending—Rawls's conception of a democratic society assigns taxation a more institutional role. In Rawls's framework, a set of institutions is necessary to ensure equal access to education and healthcare for all citizens and to guarantee that positions and offices remain open to everyone. The role of taxation, therefore, is to prevent these institutions from being undermined by excessive disparities in wealth and income. Although the function of taxation may appear secondary, its design must always remain consistent with the requirements of the social contract. That

[3] Rawls (2008, 245).

is, no individual should be permitted to benefit from the cooperative efforts of others without contributing their fair share.

This book advances the fundamental principle of fiscal democracy within a society governed by the norms of reciprocity and cooperation. We present a novel argument in support of Rawls's property-owning democracy by articulating a fiscal contract embedded within the broader framework of the social contract. This contract establishes a direct and necessary connection between taxation and its use in fostering effective equality of opportunity. It follows that justice in both the distribution of the benefits generated by the basic institutions and the distribution of the tax burden depends on the validity of the reciprocity principle, as upheld by the fiscal contract—namely, that each citizen can trust that all others are participating in a fair mutual endeavour.

In contemporary democracies, increasingly captured by market dynamics, economic and financial elites compete for electoral support while simultaneously exerting disproportionate influence over policymaking. This influence has eroded the foundations of the social contract and distributive justice, as evidenced by rising levels of income inequality and wealth concentration. In a market democracy, affluent individuals and groups operate as *de facto* oligarchies, seeking to preserve and expand their economic advantage. They do so by shaping tax systems to their benefit, exploiting tax havens, maintaining opacity in fiscal governance, curbing the regulatory capacity of the state, expanding financial privileges, exerting control over law enforcement, and engaging in strategic lobbying. As a result, a gradual transformation of the social contract is observed. The cooperative nature of democratic citizenship, where all members are participants in a shared enterprise, is increasingly supplanted by a model of market bargaining, in which individuals relate to one another as buyers and sellers. This shift extends beyond economic transactions to the political sphere, where votes are treated as commodities and citizens as market actors, thereby undermining the legitimacy of fiscal and distributive institutions in contemporary democracies.

The process through which the invisible hand of the market has gradually prevailed over the visible hand of democracy follows a well-defined historical trajectory—beginning with Adam Smith's critique of state intervention and Jeremy Bentham's staunch rejection of the social contract, and accelerating in more recent decades (see Chap. 2). This evolution reflects a deeper conflict: the opposition between competing visions of the fiscal role of the state and the public budget in addressing fundamental dilemmas of social justice. Within the logic of the market, justice in the allocation of resources between private and public goods is entrusted to the benevolence of an impartial observer—one who aggregates individual preferences to select efficient allocative outcomes, justified through a principle of equity embedded in a social welfare function. In this framework, equity has no independent normative value; it is subsumed under the pursuit of allocative efficiency. Likewise, questions of fairness in taxation are treated as unrelated to the purposes for which tax revenues are ultimately spent, a view which has historically been shaped by the dominance of the ability-to-pay principle over the benefit principle of taxation. This conceptual separation is a defining feature of market democracy, which fosters a kind of fiscal myopia: a limited view of the public sector's role as primarily one of preserving and stabilizing the property relations intrinsic to a market economy (see Chap. 3).

This interpretation of the role of the state can be seen, to some extent, as the culmination of mainstream economic thought. Market democracy implicitly combines deference to the signalling power of prices with a minimal acceptance of governmental redistribution—a residual function that rests on the questionable assumption that the unrestrained pursuit of profit in the economic sphere can coexist with the pursuit of social justice in the political sphere. Neoliberalism's success in shaping market democracy has relied on a powerful narrative: that the capitalist process, by continuously raising standards of living, is inherently virtuous. This narrative has served to obscure the problems associated with the concurrent rise in inequality and wealth concentration that market democracies often generate. Consequently, the possibility that democracy might be vulnerable to the erosion of the social contract has been neglected or dismissed—along with the risk that, once this erosion begins, democracy may slide rapidly from oligarchy into autocracy.

The deteriorating conditions under which contemporary democracies operate call for a reconstruction of fiscal democracy as a means to revitalize the social contract and counter democratic decay. From this perspective, although John Rawls's concept of a property-owning democracy may appear utopian, the pursuit of practical approximations to his model remains both necessary and promising. We propose (Chap. 4) a model of Democratic Welfare State as a pragmatic approximation of the property-owning democracy, serving as a foundation for reestablishing the role of the fiscal contract in shaping democratic governance. The Democratic Welfare State sets forth a series of minimum institutional requirements designed to counteract the effects of market-captured democracy. These foundational elements include restoring a comprehensive income tax; reasserting the importance of the link between taxation and public spending; complementing the ability-to-pay principle with a renewed focus on the benefit principle; eliminating unjustified preferential tax treatments; providing universal access to core welfare programmes; defining the conditions under which a basic income or minimum wage could be implemented; and rethinking the international dimension of the social contract. We explore how these elements can contribute to building a more inclusive social framework in key policy areas such as education, healthcare, housing, and the labour market. The objective is to establish the fiscal foundations of a cooperative democracy. Yet, consistent with the logic of the theory of the second best, these foundations must be considered as an integrated whole: addressing one condition in isolation risks producing a suboptimal outcome relative to the status quo. Holistic reform, rather than piecemeal adjustment, is therefore essential for achieving democratic renewal.

References

Rawls, J. (1999). *A theory of justice: Revised edition*. Harvard University Press.
Rawls, J. (2001). *Justice as fairness: A restatement*. Harvard University Press.
Rawls, J. (2008). *Lectures on the History of Political Philosophy*. Harvard University Press.

CHAPTER 2

The Lost Road: Fiscal Contract and Fiscal Theory in Historical Perspective

Abstract The history of the relationship between fiscal theory and the social contract marks a lost path in the construction of a fiscal democracy grounded in a fiscal contract. This chapter traces the historical trajectory through which the invisible hand of the market has gradually prevailed over the visible hand of democracy—from Rousseau to Adam Smith's critique of state intervention to Jeremy Bentham's staunch rejection of the social contract, with this shift accelerating from the late nineteenth century up to the emergence of market democracy. This evolution reflects a deeper conflict: the clash between competing visions of the fiscal role of the state and of the public budget in addressing fundamental dilemmas of social justice, paralleling the contrast between the ability-to-pay principle and the benefit principle of taxation. The benefit theory of taxation, historically overshadowed by the ability-to-pay principle, represents the lost path toward the idea of a fiscal contract.

Keywords Social contract • Fiscal contract • Cooperative democracy • Ability-to-pay principle • Benefit principle

P. Liberati, M. Paradiso, *Rebuilding Fiscal Democracy*,
https://doi.org/10.1057/978-3-032-04859-2_2

The Fiscal Contract in Jean Jacques Rousseau

The modern constitutional state and the problematic relationship between liberty and equality, between citizens and society, emerges from the Declaration of the Rights of Man. Since then, individualism and the limits to the action of public powers in a liberal society had to be reconciled with pluralism and egalitarianism in a democratic society. As argued by Benjamin Constant in his speech to the Paris Assembly in 1819, the contrast between the liberty of the ancients and of the moderns expressed the controversial relationship between liberalism and democracy, that is between the limitation of public power and its distribution in society.[1] In particular, the limits on public power defines the perimeter of negative liberty, with the aim of protecting the individual's freedom from the interference of governments; accordingly, the narrower the scope of action for those in power, the greater the possibility of limiting their abuses. The distribution of powers requires the democratic rules of the game establishing a wide dispersion of political power, to ensure both the realization of positive liberties through the broadest participation in public decision-making and the conditions to allow the self-realization of the individual, forcing the government to provide an environment of equal opportunities for every citizen. The relationship between liberalism and democracy has to hinge on how to reconcile those negative and positive liberties, that is, on how to seek an equilibrium between setting limits to government intervention while at the same time introducing positive duties to its action.

In raising this issue, Constant asserted the superiority of liberalism as the liberty of the moderns, in contrast to Jean-Jacques Rousseau's vision in 'The Social Contract',[2] where the egalitarian ideal is realized through the general will aimed at the common good. The political society in a republican democracy envisioned by Rousseau, indeed, could not exist independently of the will of individuals; so much, that it was conceived as a body created at their image. Accordingly, by voluntarily signing the social contract, every individual becomes a member of the sovereign body and, as a citizen, she shares the sovereign power with other individuals, whose task is to legitimately translate the general will into individual rights that

[1] On Constant's (1819/1988) interpretation and critique of Rousseau, see Bobbio (1990) and Simpson (2006).

[2] Rousseau (1762/1997).

must be ensured for their fullest expression and protection.[3] The political power, originated by the general will, had its limit in the guarantee that "the sovereign body" could not harm its members by imposing "chains" on the common good.[4]

Rousseau could not have imagined that Robespierre would hold a copy of 'The Social Contract' in his hands as the guillotine came down in the name of the people's sovereignty, nor that this event would have led to the harsh critiques of the 'Contract' by the classical liberal doctrine, from Adam Smith and Jeremy Bentham to Alexis de Tocqueville and John Stuart Mill. This doctrine, founded on the principles of natural law, rejected Rousseau's vision, as it did not accept the existence of laws dependent on the will of individuals; rather, it was based on the concept of the original state of nature in which all individuals were guaranteed the natural rights to liberty and property. In this context, individuals accepted to alienate their natural liberty to set a political authority, which thereby assumed the duty to preserve and defend natural rights. Thus, the state of nature became an ideal and essential construct to justify the necessity of placing limits on political power, and it was decisive for the consolidation of a liberal state limited in its powers and functions, both in the Virginia Declaration of Rights of 1776 and in the French Declaration of the Rights of Man of 1789.

It is precisely this concept of the state of nature that Rousseau, in his 'Discourse on the Origin of Inequality'[5], rejected and sought to distance himself from. For him, human nature has an evolutionary representation, moving from the condition of solitary life to forms of aggregation and cooperation, then leading to an organization of society in which the development of agriculture, metallurgy, and especially private property produce inequalities, eventually giving rise to an endemic conflict between rich and poor that dissolves society in instability. The solution to this conflict is a republic founded on a social contract, capable of reconciling power with citizenship, distributive justice with liberty, and guaranteeing the stability of the political community. Since the law emanates from the general will, each citizen, within the framework of the social contract, remains free. By

[3] For a discussion of Rousseau's aim to theorize what form a political association must take to be considered legitimate, see Cohen (2010).

[4] Rousseau (1762/1997, 217).

[5] Rousseau (1754/1973).

affirming that the political authority cannot arise at the price of liberty, Rousseau nonetheless distances himself from the contractualism of Hobbes and Locke.

In Hobbes, the conflict between rich and poor, as well as the human impulse to dominate others, is resolved through an appeal to a sovereign authority. Yet this resolution comes at the cost of perpetuating distributive injustice, which becomes institutionalized within the legal framework, thereby legitimizing the dominance of the strong over the weak. The powers of the sovereign are thus unlimited, and aimed to exercise authority over men and put an end to the universal war arising from the state of nature.[6]

For Rousseau it is unacceptable that individuals surrender their freedom to political power for the sake of peace, as in Hobbes, or to defend property as in Locke, since freedom is an inalienable right.[7] In the social contract, every individual "is contracting with himself";[8] the strength of this vision is that the social contract is a mutual pact among all members of the community that all have agreed upon, rather than an agreement establishing subordination to political power. Once the social contract is signed, if there are opponents, "their opposition does not invalidate the contract, but merely prevents them from being included in it".[9] Every citizen is therefore simultaneously member and sovereign of the political body, bounded by the contract to all other citizens in a relationship of mutual recognition of rights and cooperation for the realization of the necessary conditions for a moral liberty based on the sovereignty of the general will. Moral freedom is the realization of individual autonomy.[10] In this sense, it embodies positive liberty, achieved through laws that individuals prescribe for themselves in order to achieve equality—"because freedom cannot subsist without it".[11] At the same time, it also entails negative liberty, insofar as the law shields each person from the arbitrary actions and injustices that others may inflict upon them.[12]

[6] For this interpretation of Hobbes (1651/1991) see Riley (1982), Newey (2014).
[7] Locke (1690/1988).
[8] Rousseau (1762/1997, 51).
[9] Rousseau (1762/1997, 123).
[10] Rousseau (1762/1997, 53).
[11] Rousseau (1762/1997, 78).
[12] See Viroli (1988, 1989).

The political body envisioned by Rousseau is not the one envisioned by Hobbes, and famously depicted in the frontispiece engraving of the first edition of 'Leviathan': a sovereign whose head governs a body composed of individuals equal in their natural rights, yet equally subject to his absolute power. In Hobbes's state of nature, individuals have conflicting interests and passions; to escape mutual destruction, they join in a political society in which sovereign authority ensures peace and imposes laws which he is not subject to. For Rousseau, the political body is not personified in a sovereign: it "can be looked upon as an organized body, alive, and similar to man's"; the vitality of this body lies in the cooperation of the different organs, whose functioning is governed by the general will aimed at achieving moral liberty. The following quotation provides a vivid and meaningful image of the political body: "The sovereign power represents the head; the laws and customs are the brain, the principle [...] of the will, and of the senses, of which the judges and magistrates are the organs; commerce, industry, and agriculture are the mouth and stomach, which prepare the common subsistence; public finances are the blood which a wise economy, performing the functions of the heart, sends out to distribute nourishment and life throughout the entire body; the citizens are the body and the members that make the machine move, live, and work".[13]

This passage is taken from the 'Discourse on Political Economy', originally published in 1755 in the Encyclopédie, which anticipates 'The Social Contract'. The economic role of government is central, and "the first rule of public economy is that the administration should conform to the laws".[14] Through the mechanism of public finance, the government provides "nourishment and life" by deploying public resources in accordance with laws that are expressions of the general will. To implement the social contract, the government must translate these laws into fiscal actions aimed at addressing inequalities, and enabling the effective exercise of freedom.

This entails, the realization of distributive justice, thereby ensuring equal bargaining power among individuals in the governance of the republic. Failing that, the concentration of wealth in the hands of a few would inevitably distort the general will, producing laws that serve the interests of the few at the expense of the many. However, this does not mean that the government should act "by taking treasures away from those who possess

[13] Rousseau (1755/1999, 6).
[14] Rousseau (1755/1999, 11).

them, but by depriving everyone of the means to accumulate treasures, nor by building poorhouses, but by shielding citizens from becoming poor".[15] Indeed, for Rousseau, private property is "the most sacred of all the rights of citizens, and more important in some respects than freedom itself; either because it bears more directly on the preservation of life; or because goods being easier to usurp and more difficult to defend; or finally because property is the true foundation of civil society, and the true guarantee of the citizens' commitments: for if persons were not answerable with their goods, nothing would be so easy as to elude one's duties and scoff at the laws".[16]

The protection of property rights is essential to establishing and securing, within the social contract, the conditions for a stable and cooperative social order.[17] The aim of the contract is to pursue freedom by removing inequalities through the use of public resources funded by the contributions of all citizens. It is a *quid pro quo*, in which both the fiscal nature of the contract and the citizenship are recognized: the mutual recognition of freedom in equality corresponds to the mutual commitment to contribute to public resources. The citizens' fiscal duty thus derives from the contract, yet Rousseau does not regard it as voluntary. The scope of this duty is determined by the government, which—through public finance—is committed with implementing the contract in accordance with a majority rule, as Locke had already suggested.[18] However, the governing majority under no circumstances should deviate from the general will, within which the rights of the minority are also safeguarded.

In public finance decisions, the collection and allocation of taxes must reflect the purpose set by the contract in achieving equal opportunities for every citizen, since liberty cannot exist without equality. It is conceivable that over time different political majorities may arrive at different public finance decisions, but only within the boundaries of mutually beneficial decisions for everyone. In this contractual perspective, the tax corresponds to the benefits "that every person derives from the social confederation"[19] rather than simply being proportional to wealth. Since the distribution of

[15] Rousseau (1755/1999, 19).

[16] Rousseau (1755/1999, 23).

[17] Rousseau's support for private property was tempered by his criticism of the concentration of property in the hands of a few. See Dent (1992, 199).

[18] Locke (1690/1988).

[19] Rousseau (1755, 31).

those benefits may differently affect rich and poor, those who possess more goods enjoy greater benefits from the goods and services provided by the government. This highlights that, in a social contract, horizontal equity in taxation is of fundamental importance, as to an equal wealth, however measured, must correspond an equal taxation. This view does not imply a preference for proportional taxation; yet, it rather sets the relevance of combining benefit and ability to pay principles when implementing taxes.[20] This view implies that the possible rationale for progressive taxation lies in the relationship between wealth, as a measure of the citizen's ability to pay, and the benefit they derive from the social confederation, which increases as wealth increases. The reference to differing abilities to pay in relation to wealth becomes relevant insofar as the varying levels of benefit are assessed in terms of the different levels of public services received by the rich compared to the poor. This integration between ability to pay and benefit expresses the distinctive character of the contractualist conception of taxation within the fiscal contract.

A comparable rationale had already been articulated by Hobbes, for whom taxation represented the price paid to the sovereign in exchange for peace—its benefits distributed among subjects in proportion to their wealth, as reflected in their consumption of goods. In both Hobbes and Rousseau, the benefit principle in taxation originates in the social contract, linking private wealth to the advantages conferred by governmental action. Thus, differences in individual wealth correspond to differences in the capacity to contribute, since such wealth is also a product of state intervention. However, a fundamental divergence remains: for Hobbes, the role of government is strictly limited to maintaining peace; for Rousseau, its scope extends as far as the general will demands in pursuit of equality. Such correspondence between taxation and its use, grounded in the general will, guarantees that people "would never be overwhelmed by taxes, or would at least be consoled for the harshness of the levy by feeling confident about the use of these taxes".[21] Within the broader framework of the social contract, Rousseau acknowledges the existence of a fiscal contract, from which the notion of fiscal citizenship emerges—grounded in each individual's duty to

[20] Rousseau's adherence to the benefit principle and his reference to the ability to pay were noted by Gribnau and Frecknall Hughes (2022). However, they do not recognize the integration of the two principles in Rousseau's framework.

[21] Rousseau (1755/1999, 24).

pay taxes in order to partake in the benefits of the social confederation.[22] This would be reflected in the concrete relationship between the benefit principle and the ability-to-pay principle in taxation.

However, Rousseau did not overlook the possibility that government could betray the general will by using taxes for opportunistic purposes in the interest of a few and at the expense of many. But even in this case, the taxpayers' response would not be long in coming: sooner or later, they would refuse to pay the tax, and the betrayal of the general will would lead to the dissolution of the democratic republic.[23] The dissolution stems from a breach of the fiscal contract. It is the cornerstone of fiscal democracy, since undermining the correspondence between taxation and its use in advancing liberty through equality threatens the entire system of rights and obligations that governs cooperation among citizens within the republic. The assessment of such a rupture has been—and continues to be—shaped by divergent value judgments, rooted in differing interpretations of how liberty and equality can be effectively reconciled. Historically, these tensions have given rise to contrasting visions of the fiscal role of the state.

The Fiscal Foundation of a Market Democracy

Dismissing the Fiscal Contract

The century of the Declaration of Rights is also the time when the most radical critiques of the social contract take shape. At its core lies the assertion that the limits of state power must be grounded in the primacy of individual liberty over sovereign authority, of individual interests over sovereign's duties.

Hume and Smith were the first to be credited with abandoning the social contract in favour of the utilitarian view of the individual and society.[24] In the 'Lectures on Jurisprudence' (1762/1978) and the 'Theory of

[22] Interestingly, when the *Discourse on Political Economy* was reprinted in 1765, its title was changed to *The Citizen or Discourse on Political Economy*. See Rousseau (1765).

[23] Rousseau (1755/1999, 25).

[24] The place of Smith in the utilitarian and contractarian tradition has long been the subject of debate among historians and philosophers. Recent works have addressed this debate: see Trasher (2015) and Witztum and Young (2013). However, the position taken by John Rawls remains particularly significant: he placed Smith, alongside David Hume, as a fundamental precursor of the utilitarianism of Jeremy Bentham, John Stuart Mill, and Henry Sidgwick.

Moral Sentiments' (1759/1976), Smith follows Hume[25] asserting that obedience to the government cannot be based on consent. Instead, it is a necessity dictated by convenience, a private interest in the protection provided by the state. In outlining a history of the evolution of social institutions, Smith acknowledges that the protection of property and commerce reflects individuals' interest in establishing a sovereign authority. He recognizes that, within a system of natural liberty, private interest is aligned with collective interests in a free economy. It follows that any government failing to act in accordance with the individual interest would ultimately fail to realize the community's interest, and that only through the free pursuit of individual goal can the community as a whole benefit. Thus, he argues that in a civilized society, "man has almost constant occasion for the help of his brethren, and it is in vain for him to expect it from their benevolence only. He will be more likely to prevail if he can interest their self-love in his favour, and show them that it is for their own advantage to do for him what he requires of them".[26]

As a consequence, to ensure that individual interest is in harmony with public interest, the system of natural liberty must be based on *laissez-faire*. In this system, "every man, as long as he does not violate the laws of justice, is left perfectly free to pursue his own interest his own way, and to bring both his industry and capital into competition with those of any other man, or order of men. The sovereign is completely discharged from [...] the duty of superintending the industry of private people, and of directing it towards the employments most suitable to the interests of the society".[27] The sovereign has only three duties consistent with the system of natural liberty: the defence of society from external enemies, the protection of each individual from the offences of others through an exact administration of justice, and finally, providing those public works that could not be carried out if left to private profit.[28] Public works constitute the sole concession Smith makes to public intervention, justified by the market's inability to provide essential public goods and services to society. In doing so, he

See Rawls (1999, 20 ff.). In any case, there is general agreement that utilitarianism can be discerned in the policy analysis of 'The Wealth of Nations'.

[25] In 'Of the Original Contract', Hume argues that no government was founded contractually (Hume 1784/1987, 487).

[26] Smith (1776/1904, vol. I, 16).

[27] Smith (1776/1904, vol. II, 184).

[28] Smith (1776/1904, vol. II, 184–185).

acknowledges the existence of market failures, the resolution of which must be entrusted to the state—albeit as a necessary evil to preserve the very existence of the system of natural liberty.

In this context, taxes are conceived as a necessary sacrifice to achieve this end, and the government is expected to minimize such a burden—"to take out and to keep out of the pockets of the people as little as possible".[29] Taxation should impose the least possible burden on the taxpayer, and there is no room for taxes to serve purposes beyond those dictated by market failures. Smith's solution to the apportionment of taxation nevertheless recalls a principle characteristic of the contractualist conception of taxation: "the subjects of every state ought to contribute towards the support of the government, as nearly as possible, in proportion to their respective abilities; that is, in proportion to the revenue which they respectively enjoy under the protection of the state. The expense of government to the individuals of a great nation is like the expense of management to the joint tenants of a great estate, who are all obliged to contribute in proportion to their respective interests in the estate. In the observation or neglect of this maxim consists what is called the equality or inequality of taxation".[30]

Smith accepts both the principle of ability to pay and the principle of benefit in taxation. The combination of the two principles allows for the justification of progressive taxation, since the rich derive greater benefits from the action of the state than the poor do: after all, the rich have more luxurious carriages to protect and to move along public roads.[31] As pointed out by Musgrave, in Smith "ability to pay enters once it is seen that the rich will value the benefit per carriage more highly than do the poor".[32] Regarding the relationship between taxation and the benefits of public works and services, Smith expresses the need to link the advantages of government-provided services to specific categories of taxpayers, thereby

[29] Smith (1776/1904, vol. II, 311).

[30] Smith (1776/1904, vol. II, 310).

[31] Smith1904 (1776/1904, vol II, 216). Seligman (1894a) and recently Kim (2023) affirm that Adam Smith favoured the benefit theory and proportional taxation. Musgrave (1985, 17), however, rightly pointed out that Smith's support for progressivity should also be understood in relation to the integration of the two principles. He observed that the benefit principle can be reconciled—as in Smith's formulation and similarly in Rousseau's—with the ability-to-pay principle, whereas the reverse is not true.

[32] Musgrave (1985, 21). Within the same rationale, Smith was also able to justify the application of progressive taxation in the case of a tax on house rents. Smith (1776/1904, vol. II, 325–331).

acknowledging the distinction between special public services provided on direct demand, and general public services. This, in turn, reduces the risk of abuses in the allocation of their costs and, implicitly, limits the potential expansion of the economic role of the state.[33]

It is unequivocal that, for Smith, in a free market society, the state is subordinated to the primacy of the individual liberty over political authority, and to the pursuit of individual interests. In order to create the best conditions for the market to function, it is necessary to establish the institutions required for its protection and then allow the division of labour to ensure the efficient allocation of productive resources, thereby generating growth and social welfare.[34] This perspective reflects Smith's utilitarian impulse, as he sees the division of labour within the free market as the source of maximum prosperity for society as a whole.

Bentham's utilitarianism would go on to provide a criterion for the measurement of social welfare, the greatest happiness promoted by social action, represented as the sum of individual utilities. Bentham formulated the utilitarian principle as the sole criterion that the legislator should follow when enacting laws aimed at promoting the happiness of the greatest number of citizens.[35] In doing so, he opposed the natural law tradition, which he vehemently attacked as a "rhetorical nonsense",[36] an epithet used to criticize both the French Declaration of Rights and any conception of inherent natural rights. From Bentham onward, utilitarianism and liberalism have advanced hand in hand, setting aside any justification for the existence of a social contract.

John Stuart Mill made utilitarianism a social philosophy and an ethical guide the economic and social action of the state should be based on.[37] In this framework, the action of the state can be considered just when it aims to promote happiness, that is, the welfare of the entire community: utilitarianism thus becomes not merely an individual rule but a social one.

[33] Smith (1776/1904, book V, chapter I).

[34] Smith (1776/1904, vol. I, Book I).

[35] Bentham (1776/1977); (1789/1996).

[36] Bentham (1796/2002, 330).

[37] On Stuart Mill's fiscal doctrine see Musgrave (1985). Following Bentham, Mill was not in favour of progressive taxation, but he supported the progressivity of inheritance taxation. On the relation between Mill's and Bentham's fiscal doctrines, see Dome (1999).

Mill clarifies this point in 'On Liberty',[38] arguing that utility has ethical value because it is grounded in the permanent interests of mankind. It follows that the role of the state in ensuring social welfare should be limited to preventing individuals from harming or obstructing one another. At the same time, it implies protecting the individual from state interference in all matters concerning the personal sphere, from freedom of thought and association to freedom of opinion. Mill's vision affirms the conception of the minimal state. However, through his reference to social welfare, he opens the door to public intervention in cases where one individual's welfare may be overwhelmed by that of another or by that of a group.

Mill identifies certain situations in which the state could justifiably deviate from the *laissez-faire* doctrine. In particular, he points to cases in which the very nature of certain goods and services prevents private individuals from having sufficient incentive to provide them—as already anticipated by Smith. And since the benefits of these goods and services tend to be widely shared across the community, "to determine who is most interested in it is of no real importance".[39] This also implies the irrelevance of the relationship between a specific tax and its use, and therefore between the benefit of public goods and services and the tax burden. This separation allowed Mill to treat equity in taxation as a distinct issue from equity in public spending: "as a government ought to make no distinction of persons or classes in the strength of their claim on it, whatever sacrifices or claims it requires from them should be made to bear as nearly as possible with the same pressure upon all, which it must be observed, is the mode by which least sacrifice is occasioned on the whole [...] means equality on sacrifice".[40] Historically, this separation gave rise—from Mill onwards—to the concept of justice in taxation as a problem of vertical equity, and later to taxation based on the ability-to-pay principle. Once the principle of equal marginal sacrifice was established as the foundation of fairness in taxation, the separation between justice in tax burdens and justice in public spending made the fiscal contract increasingly irrelevant.

With the incorporation of marginal analysis into utilitarianism, the criterion for distributing the tax burden was derived directly from the assumption of diminishing marginal utility of income, as a basis for

[38] Mill (1859/1977, 223–224).
[39] Mill (1848/1909, 805).
[40] Mill (1848/1909, 804).

achieving vertical equity. From this assumption followed a sacrifice-based approach to taxation—no longer equal, as in Mill's formulation, but rather, in the renewed interpretations of Francis Ysidro Edgeworth and Arthur Cecil Pigou, designed so that marginal tax sacrifice would result in the least total sacrifice and thus the greatest social welfare.[41] On the basis of the assumption that income yields comparable and declining marginal utility across individuals, an argument emerged for reducing income at the top end of the distribution. However, this position was later refined by incorporating Pigou's notion of "announcement effects" of taxation, an idea that would evolve into the concept of deadweight loss and contemporary optimal tax theory,[42] whose goal is to design tax systems that raise revenue with the least possible deadweight loss. This means taxing goods with inelastic demand or supply, as they cause smaller distortions and thus lower deadweight loss, making the taxation more efficient overall. Taxation thus came to be seen as a diversion of resources from the efficient allocation the market would have achieved in the absence of state intervention.[43]

This view was not undermined by the alternative proposed by the renewed marginalist version of the benefit theory of taxation. The divergence between ability-to-pay and benefit taxation highlighted the contrast between Anglo-Saxon tax theory and that of Continental Europe.[44] The Italian school of *scienza delle finanze*—with Antonio De Viti de Marco, Ugo Mazzola, Maffeo Pantaleoni, Luigi Einaudi, and Benvenuto Griziotti—alongside Emil Sax in Austria and the important contributions of the Swedish economists Knut Wicksell and Erik Lindahl, emphasized the simultaneity of tax and expenditure decisions within the public budget. Although in different terms, they considered the application of the benefit principle an approximation of a market mechanism, albeit one constrained by the real-world functioning and limitations of political decision-making processes in constitutional democracies.

[41] Edgeworth (1897); Pigou (1928).

[42] Musgrave (1985).

[43] Musgrave (1992).

[44] An analysis of the national character of fiscal theories between the nineteenth and twentieth centuries can be found in Kayaalp (2004). On the relationship between *scienza delle finanze* and Wicksell's contribution, see Medema (2005).

Edwin Seligman,[45] the most influential American public finance economist—both for his academic standing and his role in tax reform efforts in late nineteenth-century America—suggested that the true purpose of the benefit principle lays in recognizing a specific and individually measurable advantage: that is, the benefits of public goods and services are attributed to the individuals who consume them and who pay a price proportionate to those benefits. However, such particular advantage should either disappear or play only a secondary role in a system of tax justice based on the ability-to-pay principle. Essentially, the benefit principle could not offer a sound basis for the actual design of tax systems. On this point, Seligman was explicit: once the inadequacy of the benefit principle as a foundation for taxation was acknowledged, only the ability-to-pay principle—that is, determining who should pay and how much relative to their income—remained central to shaping a tax system that promoted social justice.[46] As a consequence, by the end of the nineteenth century, under the pressure of growing social inequalities, tax systems in the US, and similarly in European countries, began to gradually shift from consumption-based taxes to income taxes, recognizing the necessity of progressive taxation.[47] The fiscal role of the state was not seen primarily as redistributing wealth through public spending, but rather in reforming fiscal democracy by requiring the wealthiest citizens to contribute in a way that reflected an ethical commitment to building a more just society: hence, those who had more were expected to contribute more. Taxing the rich became a social imperative, forming the basis for constructing a social pact founded on solidarity, ethical duty, and a form of social benevolence, embodied in the progressivity of income taxation whose foundation was the assumption of the diminishing marginal utility of income.[48] This

[45] On Seligman see Shoup (1968) and Mehrotra (2013a). Mehrotra (2013b) reconstructs the contribution of Seligman in particular, as well as that of Richard T. Ely and Henry Carter Adams, in providing the theoretical foundations for the American tax reform at the end of the nineteenth century. Moreover, Mehrotra (2013b) identifies the affirmation of the principle of ability-to-pay over the benefit principle as the economic and ethical foundation of the introduction of the progressive income tax in the US.

[46] Seligman (1895, 70). It is a conception that has remained unshaken, to the point that even recent critiques of the ability to pay principle still argues that the benefit principle is "inconsistent with every significant theory of social and economic justice". See Murphy and Nagel (2002, 19).

[47] Steinmo (1993); Prasad (2012).

[48] Mehrotra (2013a, 117).

allowed for the reconciliation of the ethical principle with the economic principle without contradiction. It upheld what Mill had asserted, that the utilitarian principle had an ethical value endowed with social value, a rule of universally recognized social action. However, taxing the rich to re-establish the fiscal contract was a myopic and partial view, as it focused not on what should be done with taxes, but on the way taxes should be collected.[49]

Such a view betrayed the fiscal contract and a comprehensive conception of the fiscal system, in which progressivity was not confined to the structure of taxation alone, but understood more broadly as the progressivity of state spending, aimed at ensuring the stable provision of public goods and services in order to achieve equality of opportunity. The question once posed by Constant—the tension between liberty and democracy, and the pursuit of a balance between imposing limits on government intervention and assigning it positive obligations—found its resolution within liberal economic thought, which addressed distributive and social dilemmas through the principle of progressive taxation. By privileging market freedom, the notion of tax justice was severed from that of justice in public spending. The latter came to be regarded as negligible, insofar as its fiscal burden was seen as an impediment to the autonomy of market forces and to the most efficient and remunerative allocation of economic resources. Thus, the fiscal foundations of market democracy were established.

The Transfer State

Over the course of the twentieth century, the consolidation of market democracy affirmed as the primary function of taxation and public expenditures the need to preserve and stabilize the property relations of the capitalist economy. This perspective represents the culmination of a historical process through which classical liberalism, from the 1970s onward, evolved into neoliberalism, adopting a market-centred ideological and policy framework that emphasizes the primacy of free markets, minimal state intervention, privatization, deregulation, and individual responsibil-

[49] In 1894, Seligman clearly articulated the ethical foundation of fiscal reform in support of the introduction of income tax in the US: "to utilize the income tax as an engine of reparation—a means of attaining greater justice". See Seligman (1894b, 616).

ity. A defining feature of this approach is the fiscal solution to issues of social justice, based on the conceptual and practical separation between taxation and the provision of public goods and services.

This has led to the development of what has been termed a transfer state, in which the public sector is primarily concerned with redistributing resources through monetary transfers, rather than directly producing and delivering services.[50] Within this framework, emphasis is placed on the tax-benefit system—particularly in-work benefits—as a necessary complement to labour market flexibility, which is viewed as essential to firm profitability. As Sloman observes, "in-work benefits support this accumulation regime by encouraging workers to take low-paid jobs and shifting the costs of maintaining these workers from low-wage employers to other taxpayers".[51] In this sense, tax credits and financial incentives function as a carrot for workers, helping to stabilize, reproduce, and legitimize the building of a market democracy.[52] As a consequence, although public services and benefits in kind play an important role in redistribution, their impact is often obscured in standard economic analyses. The prevailing practice among economists is to measure the distributional effects of taxes and cash transfers, while excluding public services from core metrics of poverty and inequality. This neglects not only the redistributive power of public provision but also its vital role in risk pooling and life-cycle redistribution. In this vision, the state ceases to be a producer of goods and services and is instead reduced to a mere vehicle for reallocating private resources among individuals. This approach silently combines a reverence for price signals with an acceptance of the state's residual redistributive role. The residual nature of this role stems from the inherent tension between the unbounded pursuit of profit in the economic domain and the pursuit of social justice in the political domain. As Kay argues, market democracy exhibits a near-total faith in cash transfers—an instrument that fails to challenge the dominance of individualistic values or address structural inequalities in social status and labour compensation.[53] A crucial consequence of the transfer state, narrowly focused on redistribution through transfers, is the exclusion of predistributive tasks and purposes from state action: the

[50] Sloman (2019).
[51] Sloman (2019, 19).
[52] Sloman (2019); Griggs et al. (2014).
[53] See Kay (2003) and Anderson (1999).

design of institutions and rules that address the root causes of inequality before it arises.[54] Notably, this is reminiscent of early twentieth-century approaches to poverty, which tended to frame it narrowly as a problem of insufficient income rather than a broader condition of deprivation. As a result, cash transfers were seen as the most appropriate instrument to eradicate poverty. This view stood in stark contrast to the orientation of Pigou, who supported universal provision of public goods and services, and to the position of Tawney, who argued that only collective expenditures could achieve outcomes that cash transfers alone could not deliver.[55]

It was after World War II that the concept of cash transfers gained greater prominence, and the debate around using the tax system either to compensate for or to replace market insufficiencies became widespread. This was notably marked by proposals such as the Negative Income Tax put forward by Milton Friedman and George Stigler.[56] It is important to highlight that, at that time, the use of tax and transfer mechanisms served the strategic purpose of reducing direct state intervention in the economy and legitimizing neoliberalism in an era marked by significant ideological pressures from the communist bloc: redistribution was instrumental in reinforcing capitalism as a counterweight to the socialist alternative. A group of influential economists during this period was actively engaged in affirming the legitimacy of market economy, moving away both from the central planning methods adopted during the war and from the emerging socialist planning models.[57] The neoliberal argument was that economic planning aimed at achieving social justice and greater equality would ultimately undermine both those goals and individual liberty itself. Consequently, cash transfers were primarily seen as a means to preserve a market-based economic order with minimal public sector interference. Redistribution was justified on the premise that social justice consists mainly of transferring income from the richest to the poorest through mechanisms such as negative taxation or subsidies directly accessible to lower-income individuals. However, the apparent power of these tools in promoting redistribution is limited if their use comes at the expense of public provision of services.

[54] Hacker (2011).
[55] Pigou (1932); Tawney (1931).
[56] Friedman (1962); Stigler (1975).
[57] See Harvey (2005); Jackson (2010); Slobodian (2018); Biebricher (2019).

From 1980s economics in general and public economics in particular have largely embraced these views, advocating for reduced public intervention in welfare provision.[58] In this framework, the state intervenes primarily to address glaring distributive problems (such as poverty) or to correct inefficiencies resulting from market failures—that is, when market fails to distribute resources in such a way as to maximize social welfare. The state thus becomes predominantly an insurance provider, constrained in size and scope by the market, and grounded in a narrow conception of the social contract. Accordingly, public economics does not generally consider taxes and public spending as outcomes of a social contract distinct from market demands. Instead, this normative approach is based on a general equilibrium framework, where taxes and spending aim solely to avoid disrupting the market—except when intervention is necessary to correct market failures.

It is important to emphasize that there is no independent or autonomous concept of market failure beyond what emerges from the general equilibrium framework: market failures are entirely internal to the model. That is, there is no independent normative benchmark for judging market outcomes other than the one provided by general equilibrium theory itself. Market failure is not defined in relation to moral, political, or social criteria (e.g., justice, equality, collective needs), but only in relation to a deviation from the conditions that ensure efficiency within the theoretical framework. In such a context, inequality (even high inequality) is not considered a market failure *per se*; rather, it is deemed admissible. However, when considering current proposals aimed at addressing growing inequality, an implicit recognition of a market failure emerges—though of a particular kind. It is an ethical failure, echoing the very terms in which, in the last decade of the nineteenth century, political and academic debate supported the ethical justification for taxing the rich through the introduction of progressive income taxation. Then as now, the policy instruments remain consistent with the principle of not intervening *ex ante* in the processes of wealth accumulation and distribution within the

[58] The emergence of public economics marked as an epistemological rupture in the economic discourse about the state. On this, see Desmarais-Tremblay et al. (2023).

market, but rather *ex post* through tax-and-transfer mechanisms and/or progressive taxation on wealth.[59]

The relative disinterest in distribution, compared to market efficiency, has led public economics to focus on optimal taxation as a means to define optimal marginal tax rates on incomes. Yet, even in this case—and in most contributions on the topic—the objective is to maximize a social welfare function that aggregates individual utilities within a second-best economic environment, that is, a framework where lump-sum taxes are unavailable, without considering the political processes that might shape the setting of marginal tax rates. Optimal taxation theory overlooks that society is more than the sum of its individuals, as implicitly assumed in the social welfare function. By contrast, in a social contract any justification for taxation (and progressivity) should be grounded in the vital role taxation plays in sustaining society over time.[60] Apart from the waves of pessimism expressed about the practical implications of optimal tax theory as a "highly unproductive activity",[61] it must be recognized that real-world governments are not actually the benevolent social planners that populate the world of public economics. The difficulty of taking these political factors into account, as well as the analytical intractability of a social contract and its consequences on democratic models, has often led economists to disregard their relevance within the optimal taxation framework. This is both because "it would not be at all obvious what kind of political constraint should be imposed on normative analysis"[62] and because "to constrain normative

[59] This narrow view of public economics has also been reinforced by the way academic opinions are presented in a limited number of mainstream economic journals, which prioritize highly technical and mathematical approaches that conform to a narrow, established paradigm. These approaches show little interest in understanding how the economy works, especially during times of stress and instability": Daunton (2023, 798ff.). This stance sharply contrasts with views expressed, for example, by a Nobel laureate from the Chicago School, who argued that "[O]f the tendencies that are harmful to sound economics, the most seductive and [...] poisonous is to focus on questions of distributions" and that "[t]he potential for improving the lives of poor people by finding different ways of distributing current production is ***nothing*** compared to the apparently limitless potential of increasing production" Lucas (2004, 8).

[60] Avi-Yonah (2002).

[61] Tanzi (2008, 117). For a critique to the structure of optimal taxation, see also Sugin (2010, 230), that "makes a case for moving beyond utilitarian conceptions of social welfare that are at the foundation of the optimal tax model, and that have become the dominant construct in tax policy analysis".

[62] Boadway (2012, 237).

analysis by political feasibility requirements would stifle its usefulness as an approach that informs the policy process";[63] a view also shared by Sandmo, who argues that "if the economist were to accept any kind of political constraint on the tax system as true constraints on economic policy, much of the prescriptive power of welfare analysis would clearly be lost".[64] This represents a rather nihilistic view of the complex relationship linking taxes and public spending in constitutional democracy. The fact that political constraints are not obvious should not open the door to their neglect.

The main consequence for the fiscal policy has been to focus efforts on finding technical conditions to determine the level of optimal marginal tax rates based on the elasticity of taxable income. The outcome, depending on the assumptions made, is to have top marginal income tax rates ranging from 73 to 83%.[65] From a positive (not normative) point of view, these tax rates are often considered feasible given that—just after World War II—the US and the UK adopted very high marginal tax rates; thus, the argument goes, if it was possible in the past, it might still be. However, it is often overlooked that the high levels of taxation in Western countries—from the beginning of the century until the 1980s—were mainly motivated by wartime needs (e.g., the rise of the marginal tax rate to 67% in 1917 in the US; the UK came close; and Roosevelt, in 1940, increased the top marginal tax rate to 81%; even higher rates were reached during World War II) and later—during the Cold War—by the need to backstop the socialist model of the Soviet Union, which capitalist democracies felt compelled to adopt in order to mitigate redistributive tensions posed by alternative political systems. This practice was particularly exploited in Western European countries, stimulating a sense of mutual obligation to a national community[66] and often using progressive taxes as a flag to "stave off more radical calls for industrial democracy" or to "mitigate radical demands for restructuring the capitalist system".[67]

These political constraints are consistent with the paradigm of normative public economics. The use of high marginal tax rates was—and still is—based on the idea that the state acts as a "transfer machine,—meaning it

[63] Boadway (2012, 239).

[64] Sandmo (1984, 116).

[65] See, for example, Diamond and Saez (2011); Piketty et al. (2014); Reynolds (2019); Kindermann and Krueger (2022).

[66] Daunton (2002).

[67] As reported in Avi-Yonah (2002, 1410).

collects a larger share of income from the wealthiest individuals through taxation and redistributes these resources to support the poorer segments of society. The issue concerns the selection of tax instruments, evaluated according to the efficiency criteria of theoretical welfare economics, within the exogenous (and arguably irrelevant) constraint of the existing constitutional structure of the polity. This framework formalizes the assumption of market democracy: that pre-tax market outcomes are presumptively just, and that tax justice can be assessed independently of the justice of public spending—with no reference to the fiscal contract or to the system of rights and obligations that underpin mutuality and cooperation among citizens in a democracy.

The Fiscal Contract in a Cooperative Democracy

Positive Benefit Taxation

It is within the benefit theory of taxation—the object of Seligman's criticism—that the centrality of the fiscal contract is affirmed, and this concept characterizes both interpretations of the theory: as a positive theory and as a normative theory of benefit. As stated by Musgrave, "[t]he issue, in the interpretation of the benefit rule, is whether focus is on the cost of the service rendered to a particular person, or whether it is on what a person (given his or her income and preferences) would be willing to pay".[68] From the perspective of fiscal history, the first case corresponds to the positive benefit theory, as formulated by De Viti de Marco and the Italian tradition of *scienza delle finanze*; the second corresponds to the normative benefit theory developed by Wicksell, Lindahl, and Musgrave.

In the framework of the positive benefit theory,[69] primarily elaborated in de Viti's work, that one can find the most coherent formulation of the fiscal contract embedded in public finance decision-making processes within the cooperative democracy—seen as the culmination of the democratic

[68] Musgrave (1985, 17).

[69] A study of the historical development of the benefit principle and its positive formulation, primarily in the work of De Viti and other prominent figures of the Italian *scienza delle finanze* can be found in Liberati and Paradiso (2019). On Italian *scienza delle finanze* in Italy, see Fasiani (1932–1933); Buchanan (1960); Fausto and De Bonis (2003); Fausto (2006); Medema (2005).

evolution of political constitutions. This conception of democratic public finance emerged in the final decade of the nineteenth century, and its principal merit lies in introducing marginalist utilitarianism into the theoretical foundations of public finance. It would not be until 1938 that this theory was brought to the attention of Anglo-American economists, and only in the 1960s was adopted—albeit through a questionable interpretation—by the Public Choice school led by James Buchanan.[70]

De Viti de Marco's theoretical departure point lies in the distribution of the cost of public goods– a line of reasoning initially set forth by Maffeo Pantaleoni within the framework of economic equilibrium, through the application of marginal calculus.[71] Pantaleoni identified in the budgetary decision-making process the mechanism by which Parliament expresses preferences regarding the allocation of public expenditure. Central to this approach is the simultaneous consideration of both sides of the public budget—that is, the interdependence between taxation and public expenditures—whose political dimension is acknowledged in the role of

[70] De Viti de Marco's (1936) 'First Principles of Public Finance' received an enthusiastic review in England from Benham (1934), but were instead met in the US with a harsh critique by Simons (1937), who opined that De Viti's book "is revealed to him not as a great book but as a monument to confusion". Simons's position was clearly consistent with the view of the ability-to-pay theory, and he certainly could not accept the role of the state as conceived by De Viti. It was Musgrave (1939) who offered a different appreciation of De Viti's theory, although framing it within the voluntary exchange theory of taxation. The prevailing interpretation of De Viti's thought—and more broadly, of the Italian *scienza delle finanze*—has, however, been canonized and also misinterpreted by Buchanan. It is from the essay that Buchanan (1960) dedicated to the Italian *scienza delle finanze* that a common narrative emerged portraying De Viti De Marco as a forerunner of Public Choice theory. However, this view cannot be fully accepted, insofar as it correctly focuses on the political nature of public finance decisions, but neglects De Viti's contractualist framework and, more importantly, misrepresents his thought by identifying, as historical foundations of Public Choice, his critique of democracy and anticipation of rent-seeking behaviour in political choices. In both his theoretical work and his political action, De Viti was a staunch defender of democracy and the social contract, as embodied in the political constitution. He remained faithful to these principles—even in the face of fascism, which he opposed—both in practice and through the theoretical and historical affirmation of his model of fiscal democracy in his 'First Principles'. On this subject, see the detailed and extensive biography of De Viti by Cardini (1985), and for interpretations of his thought that do not reduce it to Buchanan's framework, see D'Albergo (1972), Steve (1994), Fausto (2006), Liberati and Paradiso (2019), Fossati (2022). Among the more recent works aligned with Buchanan's perspective: Medema (2005); Wagner (2007); Eusepi and Wagner (2013); Giuranno and Mosca (2018).

[71] Pantaleoni (1883).

Parliament and the democratic procedures governing the discussion and approval of the budget. By establishing this interdependence, the approach reaffirms—within the context of marginalism—the benefit principle in fiscal theory, as opposed to the principle of ability to pay. De Viti explicitly rejected the conception of taxation as a mere subtraction or diversion of resources from the efficient uses they would otherwise have in a market free from state intervention. Thus, the visible hand of the public budget stands in contrast to the invisible hand of the market: the utilitarian dimension of the ability-to-pay theory and the economic nature of market decisions are thereby opposed to the contractualist dimension of the benefit theory and the political nature of budgetary decision-making.

The social value of public expenditure as the precondition for taxation would come to constitute the distinctive trait of the Italian tradition in public finance. De Viti recognized as essential to any economic treatment of public finance the political nature of budgetary decisions in parliamentary democracies governed by a constitutional contract. Accordingly, he rejected any consideration of the individual taxpayer's willingness to pay—that is, any extension of the market price-determination mechanism to the case of collective goods. As Pantaleoni affirmed, such decisions were made through budgetary procedures by Parliament, acting as the interpreter of the needs of the citizen-taxpayer. This did not imply a denial of the existence of an exchange relationship between taxes and public services—implicitly acknowledged through the joint consideration of revenue and expenditure—but rather a redefinition of that exchange in terms of the economic and political relationship between taxes and their use to achieve the social aims embedded in the constitutional contract. From this perspective, De Viti de Marco proposes a definition of taxation in a democratic society as the capital employed by the state for the production of collective goods: "The public wealth that the state aims to acquire is not the sum of the taxes it collects, but the totality of the services it provides".[72] For De Viti, the productivity of collective goods lies in their alignment with the needs of the community, represented in parliaments and consistent with the objectives of the political constitution.[73]

In 1888, in 'Il carattere teorico dell'economia finanziaria' and in 1939 in the definitive edition of 'Principi di economia finanziaria', De

[72] De Viti de Marco (1888, 62).

[73] On the concept of needs in de Viti, see Fossati (2006).

Viti recognizes in the political constitution the system of shared social values that translate into democratic finance. In this system, "the duty or obligation of citizens to pay taxes there corresponds the duty or obligation of the state to provide public services".[74] In public finance decisions, the simultaneous determination of public expenditure and taxation is thus an essential component of the social contract that binds citizens in a relationship of mutuality and cooperation for the satisfaction of collective needs. Consequently, the condition for the rationality of the relationship between taxation and collective goods is the participation of taxpayers, through parliaments, first in public finance choices and then in verifying their alignment with the objectives of the political constitution. De Viti develops his analysis of financial decision-making processes based on the assumption that the state is an enterprise that "transforms part of private wealth into public services", and that it is possible to recognize the existence of typical forms of state that embody the general and essential characteristics of a specific historical environment.[75] He identifies two typical forms of state: the monopolistic state where power is exercised by a dominant class for its exclusive benefit; and the democratic-cooperative state, understood as cooperative enterprise jointly participated by all citizens for mutualistic purposes.

It is the historical development of democracy that has led to the form of the cooperative state, which is the same society conceived as a cooperative venture for the satisfaction of collective needs, unattainable by private enterprise and requiring the production of public goods and services within the limits that society has imposed upon itself.[76] The democratic-cooperative state is therefore not a minimal state, and the limit of its action through the public budget lies in the democratically reached agreement for the satisfaction of a set of collective needs: "the participation of all in the administration of public affairs today makes every citizen a participant in governmental industry; all consumers are producers of public services and vice versa, and therefore between the economy of the former and the economy of the latter, no antagonism any longer exists".[77] Cooperation in the production of public goods and services is accompanied by the

[74] De Viti de Marco (1936, 113).
[75] De Viti de Marco (1888, 91).
[76] De Viti de Marco (1888, 97).
[77] De Viti de Marco (1888, 94).

reciprocity of corresponding advantages, and the relationship binding citizens to the state is one of exchange,[78] in which they contribute private goods that the state transforms into collective goods. De Viti recognizes the distinction between private goods and collective goods in that the latter must be consumed in equal quantities by all individuals, who have no incentive to reveal their demand, precluding the determination of a single market price as in the case of private goods. Therefore, since the units of consumption of the public good are indivisible, a distribution of benefits must be hypothesized. De Viti assumes that income is the best indicator of the capacity to consume and the advantage that the provision of collective goods has contributed to the production of each income.[79] The political constitution sets the system of values that the community places at the foundation of decisions regarding the production and distribution of wealth,[80] from which proportional or progressive forms of taxation for the distribution of the tax burden derive.

The proportional tax is accepted as the ideal endpoint in democracy of the exchange relationship that binds the state to consumer citizens: that is, the exchange between public expenditure and taxes as the outcome of a distribution of the tax burden based on the principle of benefit in its positive meaning, that is, not the measure of the benefit that each individual derives from public expenditure, but the benefit provided by public expenditure to the production of private wealth.[81] From this perspective, the benefit of expenditure is mediated in its contribution to forming the citizen's ability to pay, in line with Rousseau's approach and with that, seemingly ambiguous, of Smith. Therefore, the proportional tax is accepted only if proportional is the correspondence between the tax and the benefits of public goods, in an economic and social system where such a tax cannot disturb the allocation of resources for the purpose of production and capitalist accumulation.[82] However, this is a system that is realized only when economic equality is achieved in society, meaning that "the

[78] De Viti de Marco (1934, 44–46).

[79] De Viti de Marco (1888); (1936).

[80] De Viti de Marco (1888, 157–158).

[81] De Viti de Marco (1936, 116). The relationship between benefit and ability to pay also underpins the causal theory of taxation, developed by two other leading scholars of *scienza delle finanze*, Benvenuto Griziotti and his student Ezio Vanoni. On their scientific contribution, see Forte (1967, 2009).

[82] De Viti de Marco (1888, 160–161).

subjective circumstances—of each citizen are equal.[83] The realization of this condition is the guiding principle of democracy, and therefore political constitutions may provide for the adoption of progressive forms of taxation be adopted, implying a system of differentiated price-taxes among citizens for the financing and enjoyment of collective goods.

Since the choice between methods of distributing the tax burden is implied by the political constitution, it is not a predetermined economic principle that determines the evaluation of the benefit of the tax for each taxpayer. Instead, a political principle is decisive: that, guaranteed by the political constitution, of "free competition of social groups and parties, [so that] every class can attain power, and having attained it, must remain under the continuing control of the community".[84] Thus, a conception of public finance is affirmed, whose premise is the realization in democracy of the conditions typical of free competition, so that a governing group can always be replaced by another from the mass of taxpayers. The free political competition between categories of taxpayers, equally producers and consumers of public goods, implies a condition of equal bargaining power between taxpayers and allows for a democratic decision on the level of provision and the distribution of the cost of public goods. For De Viti, this bargaining process assumes an essentially political value, as public goods lack individual demand and therefore any form of voluntary exchange.[85] Only in the case of unanimous agreement among all taxpayers regarding the form and measure of the tax, "the problem of value to the individual—that is, the problem of the distribution of the tax burden—is settled at the very moment that a decision is made with respect to the problem of 'value to the community'—that is, the problem of the productivity of the public expenditure".[86] Thus, the economic significance of unanimity for determining the price-tax is understood, analogous to the mechanism of determining the single price in the market, of which, however, De Viti recognizes the practical impossibility—as already argued by Wicksell.[87]

[83] De Viti de Marco (1888, 161).

[84] De Viti de Marco (1936, 42).

[85] This contradicts the prevailing classification of De Viti within the voluntary exchange theories of taxation. See Musgrave (1939) and Buchanan (1960).

[86] De Viti de Marco (1936, 125–126).

[87] Wicksell (1896).

Whatever the form of the tax, the demand for public goods is not known, can only be presumed from income, and should correspond to the appreciation of citizens revealed in the budgetary choices made by their representatives for the production of public goods. For the productivity of the public good to correspond to this appreciation, an *ex ante* condition is necessary, which lies in the participation of taxpayers through parties in parliaments in the distribution of the tax burden, and an *ex post* condition, which is in the process of annual review and public discussion of the adopted distribution. The process of political participation and control over budgetary decisions, while bearing some analogies to market competition, finds both its guarantee and its regulation in the political constitution, which grounds the relationship of mutuality and cooperation that binds individuals in a democracy.

Normative Benefit Taxation

The political and economic character of the Italian theory of public finance attracted attention and, in part, criticism from Knut Wicksell, the Swedish economist who played a central role in the development of public finance theory in connection with political decision-making processes.[88]

In his fundamental contribution to public finance theory, Wicksell demonstrated that, given the indivisibility in the consumption of collective goods, the utility that the individual obtains from collective goods does not depend on his contribution but on that of others; therefore, the exchange relationship with the tax could only be realized when the rule of unanimity for the approval of public expenditure and tax choices was adopted.[89] A political voting mechanism was necessary to reveal citizens' preferences regarding the demand and supply of public goods. Wicksell was aware of the practical difficulty of applying such a mechanism, implying that it was necessary in reality to attempt to approximate voting systems as closely as possible to unanimity.

Wicksell introduced a political mechanism that resolved the problem of allocating the production cost of collective goods, while keeping it separate

[88] While adhering to the benefit theory, Wicksell (1896/1958, 81) rejected as 'meaningless' Mazzola's analogy between taxation and private market exchange, since individuals would not reveal their preferences without the involvement of a political process—which, however, Mazzola did not exclude (Mazzola, 1890/1958).

[89] Wicksell (1896).

from the issue of equity in wealth distribution, specifying that "justice in taxation tacitly presupposes justice in the existing distribution of property and income"[90] This presupposition implicitly assumed that an equitable distribution of the tax could only be determined as the collectively agreed outcome of a process of wealth production and accumulation capable of leading to a just distribution. It is difficult to imagine that Wicksell considered this outcome possible in the absence of the state's role in the production of public goods and services; more likely, and not unlike De Viti's position, he regarded public expenditure as the prerequisite of taxation, with such expenditure required to correspond to the egalitarian aims of the political constitution. The contractual dimension of Wicksell's fiscal theory clearly appears in the practice of the unanimity principle, or consensus test, for fiscal decisions—where public services should be voted on jointly with the distribution of the tax burden. The reformist socialist Wicksell could not have anticipated that, starting in the 1960s, his contractualist vision of fiscal theory would inspire, alongside Italian *scienza delle finanze*, the emergence of the Public Choice school. This approach would go on to exert a significant influence on political theory and practice, promoting a vision of a Leviathan-like state in which the democratic process, distorted by the self-interest of bureaucrats and politicians, tends to fuel the unchecked expansion of the public sector—an expansion that only constitutional constraints could restrain. The widespread interpretation offered by public choice theory of the contributions of De Viti and Wicksell has distorted and overshadowed their underlying democratic and contractualist spirit—one that could not possibly support adherence to minimal-state conceptions.[91]

This very spirit was convincingly identified by Musgrave in his interpretation of the Lindahl model, in which, assuming a fair initial distribution of income, tax, and expenditure decisions are determined simultane-

[90] Wicksell (1896/1958, 108).

[91] Wicksell as a fundamental source for Public Choice theory is widely acknowledged by Buchanan—most notably, in his autobiographical essay. See Buchanan (1999); for an overview of the development of Public Choice and its intellectual roots, see Peacock (1992); Medema (2000). Johnson (2005) investigated the dissemination of Buchanan's interpretation of Wicksell in comparison to that of Musgrave, whose interpretation remains more faithful to the original texts. A quantitative analysis of citations in the economic literature clearly demonstrates the success of Buchanan's interpretation. For a discussion of Wicksell's influence on the work of both Musgrave and Buchanan, see Hansjürgens (2000).

ously through bargaining between political actors with equal negotiating power.[92] The outcome of this process is a system of differentiated tax prices for the same level of a public good, in which wealthier individuals may place greater value on the benefits they derive from the public provision. This reflects the linkage between the benefit and ability-to-pay doctrines—"a connection that also appears in the Wicksellian context, where tax prices are needed for purposes of preference revelation".[93] The question of why the initial distribution of resources should be considered equitable, as assumed by Lindahl following Wicksell, nevertheless remained unresolved. As noted by Musgrave, such an assumption cannot hold in the absence of public goods, since an equitable distribution must encompass the entire allocation of resources, including those devoted to the production of public goods.[94] This issue found a resolution in the Samuelson's model of optimal provision of public goods, and alternatively in the approach proposed by Musgrave himself in his interpretation of the Lindahl-Johansen solution.[95] According to this interpretation, the choice of an optimal solution—defined at the equilibrium point among taxpayers' demand curves for public goods—establishes a price-tax rule that leads to a distribution of resources aligned with a certain conception of social welfare, embodied in a collectively shared value system.

The selected rule serves as an analytical benchmark for evaluating the extent to which alternative electoral systems or parliamentary procedures for budget approval approximate the optimal solution. This, in turn, relegates to the background the issue of identifying a political mechanism capable of revealing individual preferences for public goods. For Musgrave, any voting procedure useful for this purpose is ultimately nothing more than a democratic instrument designed to ensure competition among various social interests, comparable to public interventions intended to preserve market competition.[96] Accordingly, in the concrete application of economic science to public finance, it becomes paramount to possess a rationally grounded standard of reference, one that enables the assessment

[92] Lindahl (1919/1958) presented the model in his doctoral dissertation written under the supervision of Wicksell.

[93] Musgrave (1985, 21).

[94] Musgrave (1969).

[95] The reference is to Samuelson (1954). For Musgrave's interpretation of Lindahl-Johansen solution, see Musgrave (1969). See Johansen (1965).

[96] Musgrave (1969).

and comparison of efficient public behaviours and policy choices. The normative principle of benefit-based taxation is considered valid, provided that, alongside the principle of efficiency in the use of public resources, other fundamental principles are also introduced, expressed through some notion of social welfare: principles which are vital to the very existence of democracy and historically embedded in the notion of social coexistence. These include distributive justice and the balance between rights and duties, which form the foundation of the concept of liberty. It must nonetheless be acknowledged that the degree to which the price-tax rule adheres to a shared conception of collective welfare can only be assessed *ex post*, that is, through the procedures and outcomes of actual budgetary decisions. Within the framework of democratic public finance, the state, as conceived by Musgrave, is understood in a cooperative sense: "not as an organic unit wherein the individual is absorbed in the whole, or as a benevolent dictator who knows and meets the wishes of his subjects. Instead, I think of the state as an association of individuals, engaged in a cooperative venture, formed to resolve problems of social coexistence and to do so in a democratic and fair fashion".[97]

In Musgrave's conception of democratic public finance, the state is aligned with the democratic-cooperative state as theorized by De Viti.[98] In a cooperative democracy, citizens act for mutual benefit through the visible hand of public finance decision-making, aimed at the stable provision of public goods and services. The constitutional design is entrusted with the realization of a process of distributive justice within society—historically hindered by the allocative justice process governed by the invisible hand of the market.

This tension reflects the broader contrast between utilitarianism and contractualism, a distinction that lies at the heart of Rawls's theory of justice and will be central to our arguments concerning the reconstruction of the fiscal contract. As we have argued, drawing on the historical development of the economic theory of taxation, in a market democracy the problem of distributive equity lacks autonomous normative standing and is

[97] Musgrave (1999, 31).

[98] Desmarais-Tremblay (2021) also highlighted the significance of the concept of community in Musgrave's work, particularly in his understanding of social welfare. He argues that, for Musgrave, the moral dimension of public budgeting lies in the value that members of a community assign to the purposes of public finance, rather than in reference to an abstract social welfare function.

effectively addressed through allocative efficiency within the market. Similarly, the issue of tax fairness is addressed independently of how collected resources are employed, and regardless of the level or composition of public expenditure. Since 1980s, the absence of this linkage has paved the way for the legitimization of tax avoidance or exit from the tax duty without any corresponding withdrawal from the benefits of public expenditure, and it has shaped tax policies that tend to prioritize *ex post* redistribution measures rather than intervening *ex ante* to influence or modify the underlying processes of income inequalities and wealth accumulation.

References

Anderson, E. S. (1999). What is the point of equality? *Ethics, 109*(2), 287–337.

Avi-Yonah, R. S. (2002). Why tax the rich? efficiency, equity, and progressive taxation. *The Yale Law Journal, 111*, 1391–1416.

Benham, F. C. (1934). Review of *Principii di Economia Finanziaria* [*First principles of public finance*] by Antonio De Viti De Marco. *Economica* (New Series), *1*(3), 364–367.

Bentham, J. [1776] (1977). *A fragment on government.* In J. H. Burns, H. L. A. Hart (Eds.) Clarendon Press.

Bentham, J. [1789] (1996). *An introduction to the principles of morals and legislation.* In J. H. Burns, H. L. A. Hart (Eds.) Clarendon Press.

Bentham, J. [1796] (2002). Anarchical Fallacies; Being an Examination of the Declarations of Rights Issued During the French Revolution. In *The collected works of Jeremy Bentham: Rights, representation, and reform.* Clarendon Press.

Biebricher, T. (2019). *The political theory of neoliberalism.* Stanford University Press.

Boadway, R. (2012). *From optimal tax theory to tax policy: retrospective and prospective views.* Munich Lectures in Economics. MIT Press.

Bobbio, N. (1990). *Liberalism and democracy.* Verso.

Buchanan, J. M. (1960). *La scienza delle finanze*: The Italian tradition in fiscal theory. In *Fiscal theory and political economy* (pp. 24–74). University of North Carolina Press.

Buchanan, J. M. (1999). Origins, experiences, and ideas: retrospective assessment. In J. Buchanan, R. Musgrave (Eds.), *Public finance and public choice: Two contrasting visions of the state* (pp. 11–28). MIT Press-CESifo.

Cardini, A. (1985). *Antonio De Viti de Marco: La democrazia incompiuta, 1858–1943.* Laterza.

Cohen, J. (2010). *Rousseau: A free community of equals.* Oxford University Press.

Constant, B. [1819] (1988). The liberty of the ancients compared with that of the moderns. In *Political writings* (pp. 309–328). Cambridge University Press.

D'Albergo, E. (1972). Striking Outlines of the 'First Principles' by Antonio De Viti de Marco. In D'Albergo (Ed.), *Scritti in memoria di Antonio De Viti De Marco* (vol. II, pp. 5–15). Cacucci.

Daunton, M. (2002). *Just taxes: The politics of taxation in Britain, 1914–1979.* Cambridge University Press.

Daunton, M. (2023). *The economic government of the world*, Penguin Random House.

De Viti de Marco, A. (1888). *Il carattere teorico dell'economia finanziaria.* Pasqualucci.

De Viti de Marco, A. (1934). *Principii di economia finanziaria.* Einaudi.

De Viti de Marco, A. (1936). *First principles of public finance.* Johnathan Cape.

Dent, N. J. H. (1992). *A Rousseau dictionary.* Blackwell Publishers.

Desmarais-Tremblay, M. (2021). Musgrave and the Idea of Community. In R. Backhouse, A. Baujard, T. Nishizawa (Eds.), *Welfare theory, public action and ethical values: revisiting the history of welfare economics* (pp. 232–255). Cambridge University Press.

Desmarais-Tremblay, M., Johnson, M., & Sturn. R. (2023). From public finance to public economics. *The European Journal of the History of Economic Thought, 30*(5), 934–964.

Diamond, P., & Saez, E. (2011). The case for a progressive tax: From basic research to policy recommendations. *Journal of Economic Perspectives, 25*(4), 165–190.

Dome, T. (1999). Bentham and J.S. Mill on tax reform. *Utilitas, 11*(3), 320–339.

Edgeworth, F. Y. (1897). The pure theory of taxation. *Economic Journal, 7*(25), 550–571.

Eusepi, G., & Wagner, R. E. (2013). Tax prices in a democratic polity: the continuing relevance of Antonio de Viti de Marco. *History of Political Economy, 45*, 99–121.

Fasiani, M. (1932–1933). Der gegenwärtige Stand der reinen Theorie der Finanzwissenschaft in Italien. In *Zeitschrift für Nationalökonomie* (vol. III, pp. 651–691; vol. IV, pp. 79–107 and 357–388).

Fausto, D. (2006). The Italian approach to the theory of public goods. *The European Journal of the History of Economic Thought, 13*(1), 69–98.

Fausto D., & De Bonis V. (2003). The theory of public finance in Italy from the origins to the 1940s. *Il pensiero economico italiano*, special issue 11. Istituti Editoriali e Poligrafici Internazionali.

Forte, F. (1967). Attualità dell'insegnamento di Benvenuto Griziotti. *Rivista di diritto finanziario e scienza delle finanze, I*, 343–355.

Forte, F. (2009). *Ezio Vanoni economista pubblico*, Rubbettino.

Fossati, A. (2006). Needs, the principle of minimum means, and public goods in De Viti de Marco. *Journal of the History of Economic Thought, 28*(4), 427–438.

Fossati, A. (2022). Of public choice and Antonio De Viti de Marco. *Economia Internazionale/International Economics, 75*(4), 519–544.

Friedman, M. (1962). *Capitalism and freedom*. Chicago University Press.
Giuranno, M., & Mosca, M. (2018). Political realism and models of the state: Antonio de Viti de Marco and the origins of public choice. *Public Choice, 175*(3), 325–345.
Gribnau, H., & Frecknall Hughes, J. (2022). The enlightenment and influence of social contract theory on taxation. In R. van Brederode (Ed.), *Political philosophy and taxation. A history from the enlightenment to the present* (pp. 51–101). Springer Nature.
Griggs, J., Hammond, A., & Walker, R. (2014). Activation for all: Welfare reform in the United Kingdom, 1995–2009. In I. Lodemel, A. Moreira (Eds.), *Activation or workfare? Governance and the neo-liberal convergence* (chapter 4). Oxford University Press.
Hacker, J. S. (2011). The institutional foundations of middle-class democracy. *Policy Network*, 33–37.
Hansjürgens, B. (2000). The influence of Knut Wicksell on Richard Musgrave and James Buchanan. *Public Choice, 103*(95), 95–116.
Harvey, D. (2005). *A brief history of neoliberalism*. Oxford University Press.
Hobbes, T. [1651] (1991). *Leviathan. Or the matter, forme and power of a commonwealth ecclesiasticall and civill*. In R. Tuck (Ed.). Cambridge University Press.
Hume, D. [1784] (1987). Of the original contract. In E. Miller (Ed.), *Essays: moral, political, and literary* (pp. 465–487). Liberty Fund.
Jackson, B. (2010). At the origins of neo-liberalism: the free economy and the strong state, 1930–1947. *The Historical Journal, 53*(1), 129–151.
Johansen, L. (1965). *Public economics*. Rand Mc Nally and Company.
Johnson, M. (2005). Wicksell's unaminity rule. Buchanan's dominance considered. *American Journal of Economics and Sociology, 64*(4), 1049–1071.
Kay, J. (2003). *The truth about markets - Why some nations are rich but most remain poor*. Penguin Books.
Kayaalp, O. (2004). *The national element in the development of fiscal theory*. Palgrave Macmillan.
Kim, K. (2023). New light on Adam Smith's view of taxation via the concept of equity. *The European Journal of the History of Economic Thought*, 1–24.
Kindermann, F., & Krueger, D. (2022). High marginal tax rates on the top 1 percent? Lessons from a life-cycle model with idiosyncratic income risk. *American Economic Journal: Macroeconomics, 14*(2), 319–366.
Liberati, P., & Paradiso, M. (2019). La teoria positiva del beneficio e la finanza democratica in una prospettiva storica. *Rivista di Diritto Finanziario e Scienza delle Finanze, LXXVIII*(2), 85–110.
Lindahl, E. [1919] (1958). Just taxation - A positive solution. In R. A. Musgrave, A. T. Peacock (Eds.), *Classics in the theory of public finance* (pp. 168–176). Macmillan. Translated from *Die Gerechtigkeit der Besteuerung: eine Analyse*

der Steuerprinzipien auf Grundlage der Grenznutzentheorie. Lund: Gleerupska Universitetsbokhandeln, IX, 85–98.

Locke, J. [1690] (1988). The first treatise of government. In J. Locke, *Two treatises of government* (2nd edn., pp. 141–264), P. Laslett (Ed.). Cambridge University Press.

Lucas, R. E. Jr. (2004). The industrial revolution: Past and future. *Economic Education Bulletin, XLIV*(8), 1–8.

Mazzola, U. [1890] (1958). *I dati scientifici della finanza pubblica.* Loescher. Partially translated in English as "The formation of prices of public goods". In R. A. Musgrave, A. T. Peacock (Eds.), *Classics in the theory of public finance* (pp. 37–47). MacMillan.

Medema, S. G. (2000). Related disciplines': the professionalization of public choice analysis. *History of Political Economy, 32*, 289–324.

Medema, S. G. (2005). Marginalizing government: From la *scienza delle finanze* to Wicksell. *History of Political Economy, 37*(1), 1–25.

Mehrotra, A. K. (2013a). From seligman to shoup: The early Columbia school of taxation and development. In W. E. Brownlee, E. Ide, Y. Fukagai (Eds.) *The political economy of transnational tax reform: the Shoup mission to Japan in historical context* (pp. 30–54). Cambridge University Press.

Mehrotra, A. K. (2013b). *Making the modern American fiscal state: Law, Politics and the rise of progressive taxation, 1877–1929.* Cambridge University Press.

Mill, J. S. [1848] (1909). *Principles of political economy, with some of their applications to social philosophy.* In J. Ashley (Ed.). Longmans.

Mill, J. S. [1859] (1977). On Liberty. In J. M. Robson (Ed.), *The collected works of John Stuart Mill* (vol. 18, pp. 223–266). Essays in Politics and Society, Part I. University of Toronto Press.

Murphy, L., & Nagel, T. (2002). *The myth of ownership: taxes and justice.* Oxford University Press.

Musgrave, R. A. (1939). The voluntary exchange theory of public economy. *The Quarterly Journal of Economics, 53*(2), 213–237.

Musgrave, R. A. (1969). Provision for social goods. In J. Margolis, H. Guitton (Eds.), *Public economics: An analysis of public production and consumption and their relations to the private sectors* (pp. 135–142). Macmillan. Republished in R. A. Musgrave (1986), *Public finance in a democratic society* (vol. I, pp. 41–58). Social goods, taxation and fiscal policy. New York University Press.

Musgrave, R. A. (1985). A brief history of fiscal doctrine. In A. J. Auerbach, M. Feldstein (Eds.), *Handbook of public economics* (vol. 1, pp. 1–59). North-Holland.

Musgrave, R. A. (1992). Social contract, taxation and the standing of deadweight loss. *Journal of Public Economics, 49*(3), 369–381.

Musgrave, R. A. (1999). The nature of the fiscal state: The roots of my thinking. In J. M. Buchanan, R. A. Musgrave (Eds.), *Public finance and public choice: Two contrasting visions of the state* (pp. 29–49). MIT Press-CESifo.
Newey, G. (2014). *The Routledge guidebook to Hobbes' Leviathan*. Routledge.
Pantaleoni, M. (1883). Contributo al riparto delle spese pubbliche. *La Rassegna Italiana* (vol. III; pp. 25–60). Translated in English as "Contribution to the theory of the distribution of public expenditure". In R. A. Musgrave, A. T. Peacock (Eds.), *Classics in the theory of public finance*, 1958 (pp. 16–27). Macmillan.
Peacock, A. (1992). *Public choice analysis in historical perspective*. Cambridge University Press.
Pigou, A. C. (1928). *A study in public finance*. Macmillan.
Pigou, A. C. (1932). *The economics of welfare* (4th edn.). Macmillan.
Piketty, T., Saez, E., & Stantcheva, S. (2014). Optimal taxation of top labor incomes: A tale of three elasticities. *American Economic Journal: Economic Policy, 6*(1), 230–271.
Prasad, M. (2012). *The land of too much: American abundance and the paradox of poverty*. Harvard University Press.
Reynolds, A. (2019). Optimal top tax rates: A review and critique. *Cato Journal, 39*(3), 635–665.
Riley, P. (1982). *Will and political legitimacy: A critical exposition of social contract theory in Hobbes, Locke, Rousseau and Hegel*. Harvard University Press.
Rousseau, J. J. [1754] (1973). A discourse on the origin of inequality (Second Discourse). In J. J. Rousseau (Ed.), *The social contract and discourses* (2nd edn., pp. 3–81). Dent J.M. and Sons.
Rousseau, J. J. [1755] (1999). *Discourse on political economy and the social contract*. Oxford University Press.
Rousseau, J. J. [1762] (1997). *The social contract and other later political writings*. Cambridge University Press.
Rousseau, J. J. (1765). *Le citoyen, ou discours sur l'economie politique*. Genève.
Samuelson, P. A. (1954). The pure theory of public expenditure. *Review of Economics and Statistics, 36*(4), 387–389.
Sandmo, A. (1984). Some insights from the new theory of public finance. *Empirica, 2*, 111–124.
Seligman, E. R. A. (1894a). *Progressive taxation in theory and practice*. Publications of the American Economic Association. *Economic Studies* (vol. 9(3)). Macmillan.
Seligman, E. R. A. (1894b). The income tax. *Political Science Quarterly, 9*(4), 610–648.
Seligman, E. R. A. (1895). *Essays in taxation*. MacMillan and Co.
Shoup, C. S. (1968). Seligman, E. R. A. In *International encyclopaedia of the social sciences*. Macmillan and Co.

Simons, H. C. (1937). Review of *First Principles of Public Finance*, by Antonio De Viti De Marco. *Journal of Political Economy, 45*(5), 712–717.
Simpson, M. (2006). *Rousseau's theory of freedom*. Continuum.
Slobodian, Q. (2018). *Globalists: The end of empire and the birth of neoliberalism*. Harvard University Press.
Sloman, P. (2019). *Transfer state - The idea of a guaranteed income and the politics of redistribution in modern Britain*. Oxford University Press.
Smith, A. [1759] (1976). *The theory of moral sentiments*. In D. D. Raphael, A. L. Macfie (Eds.). Clarendon Press.
Smith, A. [1762] (1978). *Lectures on jurisprudence*. In R. L. Meek, D. D. Raphael, P. G. Stein (Eds.). Clarendon Press.
Smith, A. [1776] (1904). *An inquiry into the nature and causes of the wealth of nations*. Edwin Cannan.
Steinmo, S. (1993). *Taxation and democracy: Swedish, British, and American approaches to financing the modern state*. Yale University Press.
Steve, S. (1994). La finanza di Antonio de Viti de Marco. *Rivista di diritto finanziario e scienza delle finanze*, giugno (pp. 171–186). Reprinted in Steve (1997), *Scritti vari* (pp. 353–370). Ciriec-Franco Angeli.
Stigler, G. J. (1975). *The citizen and the state: Essays on regulation*. University of Chicago Press.
Sugin, L. (2010). Philosophical Objection to the optimal tax model. *Tax Law Review, 64*, 229–282.
Tanzi, V. (2008). *Peoples, places and policies: China, Japan and SouthEast Asia*. Jorge Pinto Books.
Tawney, R. H. (1931). *Equality*. George Allen and Unwin.
Trasher, J. (2015). Adam Smith and the social contract. *Adam Smith Review, 8*, 195–216.
Viroli, M. (1988). *Jean-Jacques Rousseau and the 'well-ordered society'*. Cambridge University Press.
Viroli, M. (1989). Republic and Politics in Machiavelli and Rousseau. *History of Political Thought, 10*(3), 405–420.
Wagner, R. E. (2007). *Fiscal sociology and the theory of public finance*. Edward Elgar.
Wicksell, K. [1896] (1958). *Finanztheoretische Untersuchungen*. Gustav Fischer, Jena; Partially translated in English as "A new principle of just taxation". In R. Musgrave, A. T. Peacock (Eds.), *Classics in the theory of public finance* (pp. 72–118). MacMillan.
Witztum, A., & Young, J. T. (2013). Utilitarianism and the role of utility in Adam Smith. *The European Journal of the History of Economic Thought, 20*(4), 572–602.

CHAPTER 3

Inequality and Taxation in a Market Democracy

Abstract In contemporary public economics, equity has no independent normative value; it is subsumed under the pursuit of allocative efficiency. Likewise, questions of fairness in taxation are treated as unrelated to the purposes for which tax revenues are ultimately spent. This conceptual separation is a defining feature of market democracy, which fosters a kind of fiscal myopia: a limited view of the public sector's role as primarily one of preserving and stabilizing the property relations intrinsic to a capitalist economy. This has shaped tax policies that tend to prioritize *ex post* redistribution measures—as 'tax the rich' manifestos—rather than intervening *ex ante* to influence or modify the underlying processes of income and wealth accumulation. Such a view betrays the fiscal contract and the comprehensive conception of the fiscal system, in which progressivity is not confined to the structure of taxation alone, but understood more broadly as the progressivity of public expenditures aimed at ensuring the stable provision of public goods in order to achieve equality of opportunity.

Keywords Market democracy • Inequality • Wealth taxation • Dual income tax • Tax havens

P. Liberati, M. Paradiso, *Rebuilding Fiscal Democracy*,
https://doi.org/10.1057/978-3-032-04859-2_3

Inequality in a Market Democracy

Since the 1980s, there has been a renewed economic interest in income and wealth inequality;[1] and the main reason for this interest is that countries of the richest part of the world experienced a rise in inequality. The levels of inequality are not homogeneous among geographical areas: in 2020, the share of *wealth* held by the top 1% of the population is significantly lower in Europe (25.6%) and Oceania (24.6%) than in North America (34.3%, with a 34.8% in 2023 in the US according to the World Inequality Database - WID); in this latter area, the concentration of income and wealth is comparable to that observed in Latin America (35.1%), Asia (on average around 35.5%), and Africa (35.8%). The concentration of wealth in the US is higher than that observed in some Latin American countries (e.g. Ecuador, Argentina, El Salvador, Uruguay, all countries with a concentration not above 25%).[2] It is also much higher of that observed in economically comparable European countries, like the UK, in which—according to WID—the top 1% net personal wealth share has fallen from 45.1% in 1950 to 21.3% in 2023 after having touched the lower bound of 17.8% in 1984; or in Germany (27.6% in 2023) or in Italy (22.1% in 2023) or in Spain (23.8% in 2023) or in France (27.2% in 2023).

Furthermore, while in the US, wealth concentration among the bottom 50% of the population has remained almost constant since the sixties (never above 2% and 0.9% in 2023), in the UK the same share—from 1995 to 2023—has fallen from 6.3% to 4.7% , from 4.3% to 3.5% in Germany, from 10.2% to 2.5% in Italy, from 6.7% to 4.9% in France, from 7.2% to 6.7% in Spain.[3] One can say that even though maintaining some differences, European countries are on the route of mimicking the US model, at least in terms of the low concentration of wealth in the bottom part of the income distribution. Analogously, the concentration of income on the top 1% of the population—on average lower than the concentration of wealth—is again lower in Europe (11.8%) and in Oceania (12.4%) than in North America (17.9%), Asia and Africa (19.3%). In the US, this concentration reaches 20.7% in 2023, compared to 13.1% in the UK, 12.7% in Germany, 12.3% in Italy, 12% in France, and 11.9% in Spain, all countries (with the exception of Spain) showing an increasing trend from the eighties.

[1] See, for a discussion, Ramos Pinto (2019).

[2] See Bergolo et al. (2023).

[3] Data are taken from the website of WID depicting country graphs at https://wid.world/.

Whether this growth of inequality is caused by the weakness of democratic systems and/or whether inequality might undermine democracy are long-standing issues, deeply investigated in a large strand of economic and political literature. A recent analysis shows that there is no robust evidence that democracy reduces inequality and also shows that "the effect of democracy on redistribution and inequality may be more nuanced than often presumed and highly heterogeneous across societies".[4] To some extent, the fact that the US and China—in 2023—have comparable wealth concentrations among the top 1% of the population (34.8% and 30.3% , respectively), and that the US and the Russian federation have comparable income concentrations (20.7% and 23.8%, respectively) show how difficult may be to disentangle a proper relationship between inequality and political regimes.

This blurred relationship between democracy and inequality might depend on the relatively low prevalence of democracy around the world, and also on the variety of available democracy indexes used to measure it.[5] According to the *Freedom House* data for 2024, 126 countries in the world (over 210) are indeed classified as 'Not Free' or 'Partially Free', and most of them are located in Africa, Asia, Latin America, Eurasia, and Middle East. The indicators used for this classification embody various deviations from the ordinary functioning of democracy, which may contribute to shape an environment encouraging income and wealth concentration. Other datasets also confirm this outcome; 140 countries out of 176 surveyed have typologies of democracy ranging from 'deficient democracies' to 'hybrid regimes' to either 'moderate' or 'hard' autocracies.[6] Moreover, the democracy index for 2023 reveals that only 7.8% of the world population lives in countries classified as 'full democracies', and less than a half of the world lives in either a 'full' or a 'flawed democracy'.[7] Even though weaker democracies might, in principle, be associated with greater wealth concentration, no clear relationship emerges: in some cases, inequality increased while the quality of democracy remained unchanged; in others, inequality declined without any improvement in democratic quality; and

[4] Acemoglu et al. (2015, 1954). For a different perspective, see Sirowy and Inkeles (1990).

[5] Krieger (2022) for an overview of existing democracy index. See also Munck and Verkuilen (2002) and Gründler and Krieger (2021).

[6] Data from the democracy matrix developed by Lauth and Schlenkrich (2020).

[7] Economist Intelligence Unit (2024).

in yet others, democratic quality declined with no apparent change in inequality levels.[8]

Alternatively, the empirical evidence of the blurred relationship between democracy and inequality might be due to the possibility that democracies are captured by the economic power. Indeed, as any market economy is embedded in a political system, both the functioning of institutions and the implementation of public policies might ultimately depend on the distribution of both economic and political power in society. It follows that an unequal distribution of power may generate an unequal distribution of resources, which would lead to a positive correlation between democracy and inequality, with greater concentration of resources occurring even in countries with a high level of formal democracy. From another perspective, the capture of democracy may prevent a negative correlation between democracy and inequality: "history has shown that democracy and tremendous concentrations of wealth are more likely to coexist than to clash".[9] The unequal distribution of power may also underlie the idea that highly unequal societies do not function effectively, as they risk being neither stable nor sustainable in the long term. In particular, when a single social group holds excessive power, it is more likely to succeed in securing policies that benefit itself rather than society as a whole.[10]

Although this capture could in principle be realized by any organized segment of the population, in more developed democracies—where the *de jure* distribution of power is more homogeneous—it is usually the richest individuals that hold the largest share of the *de facto* power. To some extent, they are rich because they succeed in controlling the political process at their advantage; at the same time, they aspire to control the political process to preserve their wealth and incomes. By adopting what is necessary for 'wealth defense' and 'income defense',[11] wealthy people act as oligarchies and usually invest resources to create favourable tax treatments or offshore tax havens, to keep the tax systems opaque, to limit the regulation power of the state, to increase financial opportunities, to control law enforcement, or to run lobbying activities. All these strategies "raise the cognitive barrier for

[8] Ansell and Samuels (2018, 2).

[9] Ansell and Samuels (2018, 15). See also Acemoglu et al. (2015).

[10] Stiglitz (2013).

[11] Winters (2011), especially chapter 5.

entry into the debate" and allows well-funded and well-informed insiders to set policies "completely behind the scenes".[12]

These oligarchies usually represent only a small fraction of the population, but their power over both the political actors and the institutions of democracy allows them to concentrate on a limited set of crucial policy issues that maximize their own benefits. This dynamic can consistently coexist with pluralistic competition in many other policy areas, yet it ultimately undermines the democratic process's ability to address market-generated inequalities.[13] This would imply that in captured democracies, inequality might be higher—helping to explain why greater democratization—does not necessarily lead to a reduction in inequality.

In this regard, the impression that most of the increase in inequality has occurred in a period in which free markets have consolidated their role as the main tool for economic and political coordination is hard to disprove. In gaining this space, free market—even though at varying degrees around the world and after the golden age of post-war prosperity in developing the welfare state—has led first to a recalibration and then to a retrenchment of universal welfare states, a deepening of the globalization process and of its competitive pressures, a liberalisation of capital movements, a shift of productive activities abroad and of profits in low-taxing jurisdictions, a limited increase (if not a reduction) of wage shares in national income, an over-development of financial activities, and the progressive obsolescence of national Keynesian-type policies.[14] As also noted, one reason why household wealth concentration was generally lower from the 1950s to the 1970s than in later decades—regardless of the need to recovery from World War II destruction—was the presence of a set of tools like anti-private capital policies, including rent control, financial containment, and nationalisation policies.[15] These are policies that at the beginning of the eighties were significantly reversed through globalization, deregulation,

[12] Naidu (2017, 121). See also Gordon (1972, 323), who states: "Capitalists will therefore be inclined to accept statutes which share the burden of taxes between owners and workers; they will favor certain kinds of taxes which permit the shifting of the tax to consumers and workers while appearing to tax capital; and they will help legitimize certain standards of vertical and horizontal 'equity' which seem to encodify some principles of justice".

[13] Winters and Page (2009, 731).

[14] See Kaufmann and Nullmeier (2021) for an analysis of welfare state developments between the end of World War II and the late 1970s.

[15] By Fessler and Schürz (2015).

and wealth transfers from public to private hands through privatization processes, stimulated by a change of the paradigm governing the economic thought.[16]

All these elements have profoundly changed the relationship between the market and the state. Without delving into the extensive literature on the varieties of capitalism,[17] it is evident that inequalities have increased with the rise of neoliberal capitalism. This rise has gone hand in hand with the ideological consolidation of neoliberalism, that has emphasized the role of the invisible hand of free markets as a source of social freedom, and underrated inequality as well as the social consequences of market failures,[18] often on the basis that the economic analysis had little to contribute on the distribution side.

The influential works by Hayek and Friedman[19] provided the economic rationale of political positions oriented to neoliberalism. In particular, the emphasis put by Hayek on individualism and free markets is thought to have been largely influential during the eighties. Especially in the UK, Hayek's critical positions on the interventionist state advocated in the Beveridge report[20] were followed up in political decisions, oriented to the belief that self-interest individuals might maximize social welfare through their own actions. To mark a possible watershed on the economic side, the award of the Nobel prize to Hayek and Friedman in the mid-seventies was a signal that the economic attitudes toward an interventionist public policy were changing: "economists now dominated the discourse in a way that they had not done so previously".[21] As a consequence, the political sphere was also influenced, through a reversal of the traditional roles of the market and the state. This effect was particularly pronounced in the UK, with Margaret Thatcher, and in the US, with Ronald Reagan, both in the eighties, later spreading in a large part of the European Union, and driven by the consensus that high taxes would have compromised incentives to work and produce. When Reagan became president in 1981, the top marginal federal income tax rate was 70%; when he left office in 1989, the same rate was scaled down to 28%. The collapse of the

[16] Piketty and Saez (2013).
[17] See Hall and Soskice (2001).
[18] See, for example, Brownlee (2018).
[19] Hayek (1944); Friedman (1962).
[20] Beveridge (1942).
[21] Daunton (2023, 572).

Soviet Union in 1989 and the signing of the Maastricht Treaty in 1992, introducing numerical parameters for the governance of public finances in the European Union, eventually paved the way to further reverse the relationship between the market and the state.

Unlike what happened in many European countries in the decades immediately following World War II and in the US at the time of the New Deal, the public sector—with few exceptions after the crisis of 2008—has been progressively reined in interfering in the functioning of markets[22], it has encouraged to keep taxes and expenditures at a minimum level, to rely on monetary transfers to the most needy rather than on universal welfare systems, and oriented to stimulate do-it-for-yourself solutions also for basic needs. In this framework, the welfare state has often been understood as a remedy to market failures, rather than being a fundamental element of the social contract. This set of policies was also fed, in the seventies, by the doctrine of the International Monetary Fund (IMF) and other international organizations, that moved to position encouraging free markets, deregulation, financial liberalisation and mobility of capital, while at the same time imposing those conditions on countries asking for assistance. This shift in the way the market and the state interact has fostered a concentration of economic and financial power, which has progressively constrained political authority, consolidating market democracy as a system captured by concentrated economic interests.

In market democracy, neoliberalism has served to conceal both the aims and outcomes of the market behind the narrative that they are essential for the survival of democratic systems. In particular, the burden of the welfare state, requiring taxes and public debt to finance it, is presented as an obstacle to the freedom of market forces and to the most efficient and remunerative allocation of economic resources. Therefore, only by reducing the size of the public sector at a minimum level, market forces can fully operate and then the prosperity of democratic systems guaranteed. However, the possibility that as a result of the market forces this prosperity could be unequally distributed in favour of the ones who have the power to influence political decisions is disregarded.

In a market democracy, the institutions of formal democracy may coexist with significant inequality in political power and participation. In this context, it may come as a surprise that, given the outcomes a market

[22] Merkel (2014).

democracy can generate in terms of income, wealth, and economic, and political power concentration, the current debate focuses almost exclusively on the *ex post* role of taxation in reducing a disturbing level of inequality.

Thus, in a market democracy, a paradox emerges: market outcomes are often deemed democratically legitimate, yet efforts are made to correct them through *ex post* tax interventions justified by ethical concerns over inequality. This paradox, however, is merely apparent, as such redistribution highlights a deeper refusal to tackle the mechanisms of wealth accumulation *ex ante*, which represent the root source of the distortions inherent in market democracy.

The Size of the Financial Sector

In recent decades, the expanding role of finance in the economy has significantly contributed to rising inequality and the concentration of economic power. Credit intermediation and stock markets have expanded substantially over the past 50 years. Since the 1980s, the financial sector has grown across many countries, albeit in different forms and at varying speeds.[23] However, financial expansion and transformation have often been associated with slower economic growth and, in many cases, severe financial crashes—most notably the 2008 crisis.[24] Moreover, the financial system has in some respects proved dysfunctional for economic growth, particularly due to the substantial volume of capital channelled into investments lacking social utility.[25] Thus, it may not be coincidental that the expansion of finance occurred in parallel with the rise of neoliberalism and globalization, without producing corresponding increases in employment. This has led some scholars to suggest that the growth of finance "seemed the last way to restore growth and profitability to the overextended hegemon of global capitalism".[26]

Whether or not this interpretation holds, there is broad consensus that financial sector expansion has not been limited to traditional banking. Rather, it has been driven largely by trading in complex financial instruments, increasingly decoupling profits from productive economic

[23] Sawyer (2024).
[24] OECD (2015).
[25] Sawyer (2024).
[26] Streeck (2016, 62).

activity. This trend has raised concerns, famously articulated by Keynes, that an "enterprise becomes the bubble on a whirlpool of speculators".[27] A recent example includes the development of Electronic Trading Networks, Automated Trading Systems, and High Frequency Trading, all of which use algorithms to exploit small price differences in milliseconds. Algorithmic trading accounted for 15% of market volume in 2003, rising to 85% in 2012—due in part to the US NMS Regulation (2005) and Europe's MiFID directive (2007).[28] These transformations may have contributed to rising inequality in several ways. First, since the 1970s, the labour share of income has declined, while the profit share has risen alongside financial sector expansion; second, inequality within the financial sector has contributed significantly to the income and wealth of the top 1%; third, the financial sector has played a central role in major financial crises, such as the US sub-prime mortgage collapse of 2008.[29]

The generation of excess returns in the financial sector has often been enabled by unbalanced market power and disproportionate political influence.[30] After the 2008 financial crisis, this influence became particularly evident: EU member states spent approximately 1.6 trillion euros on bailout packages, converting private debt into public liabilities. As a result, austerity policies were implemented across Europe to manage rising public debt, undermining public services and social spending.[31]

These developments are less surprising when one considers that the financial lobby in the EU spends over 120 million euros annually and employs more than 1,700 lobbyists.[32] They are also less surprising when considering the blurred borders between institutions and private financial companies; taking the UK as an example, financial institutions spent 2.3 million pounds directly on members of Parliament throughout 2020 and 2021, partly as payments for second jobs and speeches, and partly as donations, gifts, and hospitality.[33] Nearly 20% of members of the House of Lords hold paid positions in financial institutions—over half of them serving on economic and finance-related committees. There are also

[27] Keynes (1936, 159).
[28] Glantz and Kissell (2014).
[29] For a detailed treatment, see Sawyer (2024).
[30] Diamond and Chwalisz (2015).
[31] Wolf et al. (2014, 4).
[32] Wolf et al. (2014, 4).
[33] Positive Money (2022).

reported cases of former Chancellor of the Exchequer who have taken up senior roles in the financial sector after leaving office. Over the past decade, firms hiring former UK Chancellors experienced a 59% increase in access to government departments. Nearly three quarters of current and former Bank of England decision-makers have held private finance positions.[34]

In parallel, OECD and G20 countries have steadily relaxed financial regulation over the past 40 years. As such, it is difficult to regard the expansion of finance as either accidental or primarily functional to productive activity. Instead, it appears to reflect the passive role of many governments in the face of persistent and visible market failures. Also, nearly one-third of corporate profits in the US have been captured by the financial sector—while the broader economy was suffering from financial instability.[35] Furthermore, corporate behaviour has been shaped by the growing dominance of shareholder value theory, which prioritizes only dividends and stock prices.[36] This has driven management to make decisions aimed at maximizing these two metrics—often to the detriment of workers, innovation, and long-term investment. This dynamic is closely tied to the growth of finance and has far-reaching consequences.[37] For example, between 2003 and 2012, 449 firms listed in Standard and Poor top 500 companies spent 54% of their earnings (about 2.4 trillion dollars) on stock buybacks, and 37% on dividends, leaving little to fund investments in productive capabilities or higher incomes for workers.[38] In 2012, the top 500 US corporate executives received average compensation of 30.3 million dollars, with 42% in stock options and 41% in stock awards. Since buybacks boost stock prices and earnings-per-share, these practices serve to enrich executives while weakening broader economic outcomes—a

[34] Positive Money (2022, 31–32). This issue is obviously not specific to the UK. In 2015, across Europe, politicians and high-level bureaucrats are largely able to move freely between the public and private sectors, leading to a potential political bias towards former employees, or an unfair advantage for certain interest groups, a phenomenon known as the revolving door. Transparency International in 2015 states that none of the countries adequately control the revolving door, leading to possible undue influence on political decisions.

[35] Diamond and Chwalisz (2015).

[36] O'Connell and Ward (2020).

[37] Sawyer (2024).

[38] Lazonick (2014).

phenomenon some have described as "crocodile capitalism," referring to the widening gap between capital and labour.[39]

The widespread use of stock buybacks and executive compensation practices is not beyond the reach of political regulation; it is a matter of political will and alignment. Since the risks and costs associated with financial rents fall disproportionately on wage earners and the economically vulnerable, the real challenge lies not in taxing excess profits *ex post*, but in designing mechanisms that prevent such behaviours *ex ante*. In 2019, the IMF stressed that the financial crisis should have underscored the cost of weak regulation and the importance of international coordination in regulatory standards.[40]

Such reforms are essential to reverse the financial market deregulation that, since the 1980s, has reduced governments' capacity to manage public finances and macroeconomic policy. This deregulation has also strengthened the political power of transnational corporations and investment funds, while simultaneously weakening labour's bargaining power.[41] One consequence of this long-term shift has been the reversal of the postwar decline in inequality.[42] Another has been the financialization of middle- and low-income households through the expansion of housing loans—often framed as a way to include them in the so-called market democracy. Prior to the 2008 crisis, mortgage debt as a percentage of disposable income exceeded 129% in the UK and 105% in the US, compared to 70.9% in Germany and 39.4% in Italy, where stricter collateral requirements applied.[43] The consequence of the crisis is known: households could not repay their loans, and the state was compelled to bail out financial institutions. This represents a failure of market democracy, which was addressed *ex post* by turning to public finances—namely, through debt and taxation borne mostly by workers and consumers. The main actors in this global financial transformation have been US-based funds established in the 1970s and 1980s.[44] Over the past 20 years, these entities—such as BlackRock, Vanguard, and State Street—have accumulated vast assets and ownership stakes in a wide range of sectors. This financial capitalism has

[39] Daunton (2023, 802).
[40] Daunton (2023, 812).
[41] Crouch (2009).
[42] OECD (2009).
[43] Crouch (2009).
[44] Volpi (2024).

also been fundamental to the rise of so-called surveillance capitalism,[45] in which technology firms leverage control over information infrastructure to entrench their libertarian ideology—an ideology in which democracy is no longer deemed as necessary for markets to function.

Taxation in a Market Democracy

In a regime of market democracy, the central moral claim is that "thick economic liberties are among the basic rights of liberal citizens", a claim that, in principle, could be integrated into several prominent "left-liberal" theories of social justice.[46] Consequently, the foremost priority of justice is to ensure that "these liberties must be protected against incursion".[47] However, regardless of how this regime is implemented, it consistently prioritizes market needs over social and collective interests. Such a regime is based on the free market, whose most orthodox representation is that of a vast voting machine, constantly aggregating individuals' preferences into price signals. By focusing on preference aggregation, the free market also becomes a space where individuals are not bound by cooperative relationships, where the allocation of private resources is governed by voluntary exchanges and productive activities, and where the balance between private and public goods is—at best—left to the benevolence of an impartial observer. In public economics, this impartial observer is assumed to know and aggregate individual preferences in order to select efficient allocative outcomes, justified by some principle of fairness. This principle, in turn, is typically embodied in a social welfare function, in which each individual's utility is weighted and compared according to a normative value judgment.

Within this theoretical framework, the traditional allocation and distribution functions of the public sector are conceptually separated. Distributive justice holds no intrinsic or independent normative status; it is considered only after market-generated allocative efficiency has been achieved, and only in those instances where the "impartial observer" judges the resulting distribution of resources to be in need of correction. This perspective delineates a narrowly confined role for state intervention,

[45] Zuboff (2019).
[46] Tomasi (2012, 121).
[47] Arnold (2014, 240).

which is justified solely in cases of market failure. It leaves no room for a social contract—nor for a fiscal contract—that might assign broader responsibilities to the public sector beyond correcting inefficiencies. In this perspective, the social contract is *de facto* absent: it is subsumed within the market equilibrium, which is treated as the optimal expression of collective agreement regarding the allocation of both private and public resources. In other words, the market is seen as not requiring a social contract, since the economic dimension—governing production and consumption exchanges—is presumed to exhaust the terms of social relations among individuals.

Taxation plays a limited role, as it is perceived to undermine market efficiency. Consequently, the relationship between taxation and public expenditure is disregarded, and the benefits of public spending are excluded from considerations of distributive justice. If one accepts the internal logic of this system, the issue of inequality becomes effectively irrelevant: disparities in the distribution of resources are viewed merely as the natural outcome of market-based allocation mechanisms. While redistribution may occur *ex post* to reduce inequality, the normative question of what constitutes a fair distribution is subordinated to the prior objective of achieving allocative efficiency, rather than being addressed through a mutually agreed social contract. As also noted, equality should not be extracted from the economy at the expense of efficiency; rather, it ought to be embedded within the very structure of the production process.[48] This raises a critical question: if the democratic regime endorses or acquiesces to market mechanisms that produce such inequalities, on what grounds should those inequalities be corrected *ex post*?

A fundamental contradiction emerges within this framework: on the one hand, there exists a widespread belief that the market represents the optimal arena for reconciling individual interests; on the other hand, when those individual interests generate levels of inequality deemed excessive—by ethical, moral, or social standards—a collectively endorsed corrective response becomes necessary. This conception of public intervention aligns with the paradigms of public economics, in which efficiency is prioritized, and distributive concerns are addressed *ex post*, subject to an equity criterion. Taxation emerges as the primary instrument for mitigating inequality—only when it is retrospectively acknowledged that market

[48] Matzner and Streeck (1991, 16).

outcomes have produced socially unacceptable disparities. However, in this context, taxation serves to obscure a deeper issue: the failure of democratic institutions to regulate markets *ex ante*, or to adhere to a social contract capable of preventing such inequalities from arising in the first place. Moreover, within a regime of market democracy, there appears to be no genuine commitment to a social contract that would redefine the relationship between the market and the state in more egalitarian terms. Consequently, it is unsurprising that in economic discourse surrounding the need for taxation as a remedy for market-induced inequalities, there is little to no consideration of how such outcomes might be pre-empted through earlier institutional or normative interventions.

This intellectual framework shapes taxes and public spending not as foundational elements of social coexistence, but primarily as instruments of compensation for market dysfunctions. The recent 'Tax the Rich' campaign exemplifies this perspective, in continuity with the ideology of the earlier movement that motivated the introduction of a progressive income tax in the nineteenth century;[49] whether deliberately or unknowningly, it suggests that taxes function chiefly as compensatory mechanisms to address market failures, or to redress the privileges that a captured public sector has conferred upon the wealthiest segments of the population. The notion of compensatory taxation is deeply embedded within the concept of market democracy; mirroring the assumptions of normative public economics, the public sector is expected to intervene only upon market failure. The persuasive power of taxation's compensatory function also resonates strongly with public opinion, which is fuelled by appealing, and in many ways legitimate, notions of tax justice: the wealthy possess excessive resources, and something must be taken from them. This widespread consensus is unsurprising; however, it raises the question of whether such a principle constitutes a robust and sustainable foundation for a tax system that aspires to be a fundamental element of the social contract.

Undoubtedly, the emergence of such popular sensibilities—even when they encompass divergent views—represents a democratic achievement.[50] Nevertheless, the very fact that citizens must voice these demands, particularly after governments have permitted persistent inequalities, signals a democratic failure. As also noted, it is politically myopic to analyse justice

[49] See par. 2.2.1.
[50] Scheve and Stavasage (2016).

in taxation without concurrently examining how property and wealth are generated.[51] This shifts attention toward the causes of inequality's emergence, a concern that arguably deserves greater emphasis than debates on how inequality should be remedied.

A democracy founded on a social contract should *ex ante* prevent the excessive concentration of power, which constitutes the most direct pathway to fairness. Indeed, a social contract can flourish by averting the domination of economic and, political life by a small segment of society. In democracy, the social contract ought to channel market forces so as to equilibrate the distribution of bargaining power among various actors. From this perspective, the debate concerning government intervention versus market freedom risks becoming sterile. More fundamental is a discussion centred on power and its distribution—specifically, on who holds power and how it is exercised. Addressing this issue requires a social contract that is shared by all participants, aimed at curbing the disproportionate influence of "giant corporations, big banks, and wealthy individuals with enough resources to be heard".[52] Such actors employ their wealth to acquire lobbyists, campaign contributions, public relations efforts, legions of experts and studies, armies of lawyers, and quiet promises of future employment. These practices effectively transform the invisible hand of the market into a "wealthy and muscular arm", thereby intertwining economic dynamics with concentrated power. In most cases, the fundamental cause of rising inequality should not be attributed solely to globalization *per se*, but rather to the manner in which unequal rules—and arguably a neglected social contract—have been embedded within the very foundations of the free market.[53]

The current debate, by concentrating predominantly on taxing the rich as a panacea for socio-economic problems, risks obscuring the imperative to address pre-distributive mechanisms—that is, the ways in which markets are structured and regulated to shape initial allocations of economic power. This concern echoes Henry Simons' observation during the New Deal era—though he was certainly not opposed to market principles—that an exclusive focus on taxing the wealthy risks focusing on fabulous incomes and estates in a way leading to forgot to tax the large ones at all.[54]

[51] Murphy and Nagel (2002).
[52] Reich (2015, 82).
[53] Reich (2015, 11ff).
[54] Simons (1938, 218).

Similarly, contemporary "tax the rich" initiatives may inadvertently provide the affluent with an opportunity to divert attention from the necessity of reforming the underlying mechanisms that govern the distribution of economic power. In other words, the challenge is not merely one of *ex post* redistribution, but of dispersing economic and political power *ex ante*.[55] Within this framework, economic policies that rely solely on taxing the rich cannot constitute a sustainable solution if democratic governance remains subordinated to market forces. As previously noted, when excessive concentration of wealth and income in the hands of a few is deemed immoral or unethical, the appropriate response is to prevent such concentrations from arising in the first place. However, since markets are not reliable arbiters for correcting their own failures,[56] the flourishing of democracy requires a social contract that effectively rebalances social, economic, and political power. This necessity arises in part because the wealthy possess both economic resources and political influence that can be deployed to evade taxation—such as through threats of capital flight—thus undermining equitable fiscal policy.

This issue has not been adequately addressed in recent economic debates. Although it is widely acknowledged that inequality and tax systems are deeply intertwined with democracy,[57] the proposed solutions often appear to be misguided. Without a fundamental restructuring of the system that governs the relationship between the market and the state, it will be difficult to effectively and permanently correct market failures through taxation. As will be discussed further below, we contend that, in the absence of a social contract aimed at rebalancing the power dynamics between the market and the state, meaningful progress cannot be achieved—whether through progressive income taxation, wealth taxes, or regulatory instruments that remain vulnerable to market capture. Thus, the central issue is not merely that democracies fail to tax the rich despite high levels of inequality; rather, it is that inequality persists and intensifies when democracies collude with market power. As Rousseau insightfully noted, "the worst has already happened, when there are poor people to defend, and rich people to restrain".[58]

[55] Weale (2013).
[56] Kellee (2007).
[57] See Saez and Zucman (2019).
[58] Rousseau (1755/1999, 21).

The Paradoxes of Taxation in Market Democracy

In market democracy, the dominant economic narrative elevates taxes to a quasi-fetish status, aligning proponents of free markets and advocates for taxing the wealthy—whether they be patriotic millionaires or reformists motivated by ethical and moral concerns. However, the reality is more complex and paradoxical. While taxes—particularly on extreme wealth—are championed as tools to correct *ex post* the distribution of wealth, tax systems frequently are designed to *ex ante* facilitate the accumulation of that very wealth. In this context, the issue extends beyond tax evasion, which undeniably has significant effects, to encompass the implementation of numerous preferential tax regimes benefiting selected groups of taxpayers. This results in a fragmented tax system characterized by differentiated treatments granted to privileged minorities who possess sufficient influence to shape political decisions on tax policy.

This exit from the tax system can occur either by remaining within a country's borders or by relocating assets and capital to tax havens. The process of globalization has substantially increased the feasibility of such exits, while simultaneously exacerbating the internal fragmentation of national tax systems. James Buchanan had evidently not taken fiscal exit into account in his representation of democracy as a political market governed by opportunistic behaviour analogous to that found in economic markets, while asserting the superiority of the latter in terms of freedom and outcomes.[59] In an economic market, where efficient resource allocation is ensured through competition, exit is always feasible. In contrast, within the political market—constrained by the geographic and political borders of a democratic state—exit is typically limited to emigration, revolt, or secession. This, however, overlooks the fact that in a market democracy, exit can effectively take place through the creation of preferential tax treatments for certain categories of taxpayers. As recently observed, "crack-up capitalists spot signs of the mutation of the social contract and ask whether they could accelerate and profit from the dynamics of dissolution".[60] Practices such as wealth taxation, reliance on dual income tax systems, and the creation of tax havens—topics to be examined in subsequent paragraphs—epitomize the fiscal unravelling of the social contract.

[59] Buchanan and Faith (1989); Buchanan (1994).
[60] Slobodian (2023, 4).

Taxing Wealth

The considerable confidence placed in the feasibility of taxing wealth appears to underestimate its inherent complexity and to overstate its likelihood of success. From this perspective, it is unconvincing to assert that "a progressive wealth tax is possible because, in contrast to taxable income, which is artificially reduced, wealth is well defined at the very top".[61] Consequently, we do not consider a wealth tax the appropriate response to rising wealth inequalities, particularly when such inequalities stem from the capture of democratic institutions and a quasi-oligarchic concentration of power by the wealthiest 1% of the population.[62] This scepticism is reinforced by the recognition that wealth accumulation often results from prior, excessive accumulation of income.

Our argument does not intend to engage in the extensive debate on the advantages and drawbacks of wealth taxation.[63] What matters for the purposes of our analysis is that the wealth tax currently under discussion is primarily targeted at the super-rich. Therefore, the evaluative criteria applicable to such a tax differ significantly from those relevant to a general, recurrent wealth tax applied across the whole population. A preliminary assessment is required to understand why a wealth tax of this nature should be considered an effective instrument for reducing inequality.

Among the most frequently cited justifications for a wealth tax, the idea that wealth concentration is *per se* harmful tends to prevail over alternative rationales, such as compensating for the inadequacies of the income tax in measuring ability to pay, or correcting the intergenerational transmission of wealth. In the former case, a wealth tax would serve primarily to supplement non-comprehensive income taxation, thereby contributing to a more accurate assessment of ability to pay. However, this rationale would imply the need for a general wealth tax, rather than one restricted to the super-rich, since equal incomes combined with unequal wealth indicate differing abilities to pay across all income groups. In the latter case, when the aim is to correct inherited inequality, estate or gift taxation would appear to be a more appropriate instrument, grounded in the principle that the accident of birth should not determine life outcomes.

[61] Saez and Zucman (2019, 149).

[62] Piketty (2013); Audard (2023).

[63] For a recent survey see Adam and Miller (2020).

The proposed wealth tax, by contrast, appears to primarily target the negative externalities associated with the accumulation of wealth. Since these externalities are seen as arising from the excessive accumulation of wealth by the super-rich, a tax focused on this group may be considered justified. In this sense, it is plausible to regard such a tax as a Pigovian tax, insofar as it seeks to impose a levy on the source of the negative externality. However, this analogy implicitly assumes that any potential positive externalities resulting from capital accumulation can be disregarded in the design of the tax. The negative externality is conceptually tied to the notion that, for the very wealthy, the value of wealth extends beyond its consumption utility, implicitly challenging the principle of diminishing marginal utility of income—an idea that often underpins arguments for tax progressivity.

From a different angle, the Pigovian rationale for taxation might apply only to excessive inequality—namely, inequality that exceeds the level deemed acceptable in a well functioning market democracy. Such excessive inequality may arise in contexts marked by restricted access to economic and social opportunities, unequal political influence, heightened social conflict, and greater opportunities for legal tax avoidance.[64] Given that affluent individuals are more likely to influence political outcomes, to access decision-making bodies, and to run for public office themselves,[65] the extreme concentration of wealth and power could be viewed as inherently undemocratic. If this is the case, corrective interventions may be required at the institutional level—within the democratic framework itself—regardless of whether a wealth tax is the chosen policy instrument.

Even setting aside these broader considerations, there are specific practical concerns that raise doubts about the feasibility of implementing this particular form of wealth tax. As argued in the context of the US, the principal objective of a wealth tax should be to tax the value of financial assets, given that 80% of wealthy Americans hold listed equities, bonds, and shares in collective investment funds.[66] According to this proposal, implementation would be relatively straightforward, as these assets generally have accessible market values. Where market values are not readily available, it is suggested that tax payments be allowed in kind—that

[64] Bankman and Shaviro (2014).
[65] Fleischer (2017, 271).
[66] Saez and Zucman (2019, 150).

is, by transferring a percentage of the relevant shares, equivalent to the tax owed, directly to the tax authorities. A dedicated commission would then sell these shares to the highest bidder on the open market.

Although in-kind taxation has historical precedents—back to the Bible—[67] it is difficult to envision this mechanism functioning without significant practical challenges. For instance, it remains unclear what would occur if the highest bid received is lower than the market value assessed at the time of payment. Similarly, questions arise as to why the public sector should be exposed to the volatility of market prices—particularly if the sales must be staggered—or why it should bear the burden of constructing valuation mechanisms in cases of dispute. Moreover, it is uncertain who, aside from other wealthy individuals or large corporations, would be in a position to purchase large volumes of shares on the open market. Additional unresolved issues include whether the tax should apply to gross or net market values, and whether prior income taxes paid on returns from the same wealth should be taken into account in calculating the tax liability.

Taxing wealth on the basis of share value also implicitly amounts to taxing the imputed income derived from wealth on an accrual basis. As will be discussed below, such an approach requires assumptions regarding the nature and measurement of the imputed income to be taxed. Furthermore, extremely high levels of wealth are associated with market power. In imperfect capital markets, wealthy corporations may be able to influence share prices, making market valuations endogenous to the very wealth that is subject to taxation. These examples may represent only the tip of the iceberg when it comes to identifying an appropriate market value that could serve as a common basis for tax purposes. Moreover, the assumption that forms of wealth other than equities are negligible among the very wealthy may simply reflect the fact that such assets have, until now, been subject to relatively low levels of taxation. As part of the potentially significant behavioural responses triggered by a wealth tax, individuals may shift their holdings into untaxed or lightly taxed asset classes. Consequently, unless the wealth tax is comprehensive in scope, it may reproduce the very problems that have long affected income taxation. If certain forms of wealth are exempted, taxpayers may alter the composition of their wealth holdings to minimize their tax liabilities, thereby undermining both equity and efficiency.

[67] See Bearer-Friend (2021).

Taxing the wealth of the very rich is fundamentally different from taxing the wealth of ordinary people. While certain assets—such as immovable property or bank deposits—may be relatively easy to assess and tax under specific conditions, other assets pose considerable challenges. These include art and antiques, crypto-assets (which represent the new frontier in wealth holding), and other non-financial assets that are both difficult to value and difficult to trace. Determining whether items such as artworks, yachts, and other luxury goods should be classified as personal assets or as property held through legal entities adds further complexity, with significant implications for the effectiveness of a wealth tax. While the digitalization of financial systems has made transactions more traceable, it has also made it easier for taxpayers to remain anonymous.[68] Finally, there remains the unresolved and non-trivial issue of jurisdiction: specifically, which tax authority is entitled to tax individuals who possess wealth across multiple countries.

In line with this reasoning, we find it more plausible that, for both the moderately well-off and the super-rich, practical and political obstacles would impede the application of a wealth tax to all forms of wealth. Consequently, “a tax that applied only to some assets, and that was based on shaky valuations or was easily circumvented would create distortions and complexity, and struggle to achieve revenue and distributional objectives or political acceptance”.[69] While these issues can be addressed, their resolution depends on sufficient political will. However, if such political will does exist, it may be more appropriate to focus efforts on tackling the structural causes of inequality rather than merely mitigating its consequences through an imperfect tax instrument. Otherwise, the tax system risks perpetually chasing avoidance strategies—a dynamic that cannot serve as a stable or sustainable long-term equilibrium.

It is also important to acknowledge the implicit assumption that often underpins proposals to tax wealth: namely, that taxing capital income is no longer feasible. Yet a preliminary observation regarding the rationale for a wealth tax is that, were governments able to effectively tax all sources of capital income, a wealth tax might be unnecessary.[70] Conversely, if all forms of wealth could be reliably identified, valued, and taxed, then the need for a

[68] Güçeri and Slemrod (2023).
[69] Adam and Miller (2020, 30).
[70] See, recently, Bastani and Waldenström (2023).

capital income tax could likewise diminish. In this view, capital income taxation and wealth taxation are functionally alternative tools. However, the core issue lies in the assumption that a wealth tax could operate effectively in contexts where capital income taxation is considered unworkable. This is problematic. There is, moreover, a fundamental difference between the two taxes in the presence of heterogeneous returns. A wealth tax can only be levied in a manner that corresponds to a presumed 'normal' return on assets, whereas a capital income tax can target 'excess' returns as well. In other words, the same asset may generate widely varying levels of income across different individuals or uses—a scenario in which the theoretical equivalence between wealth taxation and capital income taxation breaks down.

Given that the primary objective of the proposed wealth tax is to reduce inequality and the concentration of wealth, it is arguable that such a tax may not be the most appropriate instrument. From an equity standpoint, what should be more heavily taxed in the hands of the super-rich is not the normal return to capital, but rather the excess returns, including those realized through capital gains. In this respect, some authors have suggested that the Achilles' heel of taxing the wealthy lies in the treatment of capital gains—not in taxing the stock of wealth *per se*.[71] Capital gains are highly concentrated among the richest individuals, and although designing an effective system for taxing them—whether on an accrual basis or upon realization—remains technically and administratively challenging, it may not be more challenging than taxing wealth. Thus, if efforts are to be made in addressing wealth inequality through taxation, it would be more effective to focus on the architecture of capital gains taxation rather than on wealth taxation, for example, through aligning the corporate income tax rate to the highest marginal rate of the personal income tax.[72]

The historical experience with national-level wealth taxes has generally been discouraging. When not carefully designed, such taxes tend to be vulnerable to avoidance—whether through legal tax planning or outright evasion.[73] Furthermore, as has been recently observed, the incompleteness of the wealth tax base can undermine its perceived legitimacy, contributing

[71] Slemrod and Chen (2023).

[72] Kopczuk (2023). This proposal is the opposite of what happens within a dual income tax system, where the corporate income tax should be aligned with the lowest marginal tax rate.

[73] Bastani and Waldenström (2023).

to the failure of many national attempts to implement it. This has often been exacerbated by the proliferation of exemptions and preferential treatments for specific asset classes. These carve-outs have been justified on various grounds, including liquidity constraints, the promotion of entrepreneurship and investment, administrative difficulties in valuation, social policy objectives, and the preservation of cultural heritage. Instruments such as trusts, usufructs, and foundations have also been commonly used to shield wealth from taxation.[74]

Since the focus of the proposed wealth tax is on the wealthiest segment of the global population, it is likely that such challenges would be magnified, casting further doubt on the tax's capacity to effectively reduce inequality. Thus, notwithstanding the theoretical appeal and growing interest in wealth taxation, its practical implementation remains deeply problematic. More fundamentally, there is the question of whether this is the appropriate tool to contrast growing inequality without simultaneously addressing the underlying mechanisms of capital accumulation that shape market democracies. The debate over whether to rely on a wealth tax or an income tax to curb inequality also risks obscuring the foundational role of taxation: namely, to finance social rights and the core institutions of a democratic society. The illusion that inequality can be meaningfully reduced simply by targeting the richest taxpayers may, in the end, fall short of seriously challenging the structural concentration of wealth.

The Questionable Rationality of the Dual Income Tax

In some cases, the ordinary functioning of tax systems appears to conflict with the claim that taxes on very large amounts of wealth are necessary to reduce inequality. The dual income tax (DIT) system, adopted in many advanced economies over the past 30 years, exemplifies this paradox. As argued,[75] the economic rationale underpinning a DIT system in small open economies is that taxing capital income is suboptimal, given that such economies face an infinitely elastic supply of capital. This condition implies the risk of significant capital flight, which could lead to inefficiently low capital intensity in production and ultimately shift the tax burden onto

[74] Perret (2021, 552).
[75] See Sørensen (1994, 2005) and Cnossen (2000).

domestic wage earners. Consequently, a lower (or even zero) tax rate on capital income is advocated to mitigate this risk.

However, this policy prescription assumes that international coordination to uphold a certain level of capital taxation is not a feasible option.[76] A low tax on capital income is therefore considered optimal only in the absence of political willingness or capacity to coordinate markets. Were such coordination achievable, capital mobility would decrease, capital tax bases would become less elastic, and higher taxation could be imposed without adverse effects. Moreover, although it is often overlooked in the literature, DIT models regard a lower tax rate on capital income as optimal only insofar as the required revenue to finance public goods and services is instead raised from less elastic tax bases—typically labour income and consumption. This implies that the notion of optimality rests on the assumption that reducing taxes on capital income, for reasons of efficiency, would not affect the level of public spending. Alternatively, if public expenditure were to decrease, the assumption is that this would not impair the generation of capital income. In other words, the framework does not account for the possibility that the goods and services essential for capital to yield returns might themselves be jeopardized in the absence of adequate taxation.

Not least, while the lower tax on capital income is generally proportional in DIT systems, the practical implementation often retains a progressive tax schedule on labour income. This is justified on the grounds that higher tax rates on labour income do not trigger a comparable flight of wage earners. However, the notion of progressivity within a DIT system differs fundamentally from its meaning within a social contract framework. Although this issue will be addressed in greater detail below, it is important to note from the outset that in a DIT framework, progressivity cannot be straightforwardly interpreted as a differential price that taxpayers pay for equal access to public goods and services based on the benefit principle—the cornerstone of the social contract that links tax revenue with public expenditure. Instead, progressivity in the DIT model emerges as a compensatory mechanism: a way to offset the loss of tax revenue from more mobile bases, such as capital, which cannot be taxed effectively.

Given that, under a DIT scheme, a significant portion of total income is subject to proportional taxation and horizontal equity is often compro-

[76] Sørensen (2005, 563).

mised, the very idea of vertical equity becomes problematic—especially when applied selectively to specific income categories. As a result, progressivity ceases to serve its traditional role as the fair price for public goods and instead becomes a technical instrument used to extract as much tax as possible from the income sources that remain sufficiently immobile to be taxed at graduated rates.

This raises a deeper question: what if all tax bases were highly elastic? In standard analyses of redistribution, the effects of tax-and-transfer systems are measured by the difference between market income and disposable income. Yet, the existence of market income is hypothetical and logically unsustainable; in reality, no kind of income can be produced without the existence of the state and the provision of public goods and services.[77]

This calls into question the conceptual foundation of the DIT model. As recently noted, speaking "of 'before' and 'after' with regard to government's role in economic life, while it has a certain kind of brisk initial plausibility, is on further investigation merely mystifying".[78] A similar perspective is shared by other authors, who argue that "given that an individual's market earnings will typically depend on a background of legal, social, and physical infrastructure—from contract enforcement to public roads—which itself depends on the tax system, it is not as if there exists some kind of normatively privileged possible world in which we somehow can have the benefits of the tax system without being taxed, and against which we should set the normative benchmark of our property entitlements".[79]

These arguments, however, are largely overlooked within the framework of a DIT system. Ultimately, DIT merely extends to personal incomes the well-known efficiency principle that it is preferable to tax less elastic rather than more elastic bases. While this reasoning may be acceptable in the context of taxing consumption goods—where individuals face uniform tax rates and can more readily adjust to changes in relative prices—it becomes far more contentious when applied to income taxation. Under DIT, incomes of equal monetary value are taxed differently based solely on their source, and revenue collection increasingly relies on income categories with lower bargaining power. This approach is at odds with

[77] Winters and Page (2009).
[78] O'Neill (2020, 71).
[79] Murphy and Nagel (2002, 72).

the basic principle of horizontal equity and raises significant concerns when viewed through the lens of the social contract, which holds that taxes should finance public goods whose benefits are equally accessible to all taxpayers—including capital owners—regardless of income type. The economic justification that capital should be taxed less—whether due to its mobility or, more controversially, its ability to exert "blackmail" on the tax system—illustrates how market democracy tends to unequally distribute bargaining power among different income groups. This disparity is particularly troubling in democratic societies, where the distribution of bargaining power shapes not only labour relations but also the architecture of the tax system itself. Income groups with lower bargaining power are less able to resist adverse tax outcomes, and this imbalance, when accepted or institutionalized, contributes directly to structural inequality. In this sense, the very design of the ordinary tax system becomes a source of inequality.

This leads to a paradox: the widespread calls for compensatory tax measures—such as wealth taxes or increased progressivity—are themselves symptomatic of the inadequacies of the ordinary tax framework. Rather than continuously adjusting the system through ad hoc corrections, a more coherent solution would be to reform the underlying structure to prevent such inequalities from arising in the first place. Yet such reform is rare. The reason is relatively straightforward: contemporary tax systems often reflect and reinforce the logic of market democracy. In doing so, they deliberately provide more powerful taxpayers with viable exit options—legal and institutional mechanisms through which they can shield themselves from full tax liability. These exit strategies are maintained and normalized through a form of institutional inertia. The internal fragmentation of tax systems, through the creation of preferential regimes or "special zones" within a country, complements the global phenomenon of tax havens. In both cases, democratic accountability is minimized in order to construct an economic environment favourable to capital, stripped of the obligations typically associated with sustaining a welfare state.[80]

Tax Havens

A "supply" of tax havens exists because there is a corresponding "demand" for them; in this sense, tax havens are a structural feature of the market

[80] Slobodian (2023).

democracy. The term gained widespread use after World War II, when it was employed to justify the sovereign right of governments to support competitive sectors of their economies in global markets.[81]

The list provided by the Corporate Tax Haven Index for 2024 is revealing: currently, the most significant facilitators of tax abuse are not marginal island jurisdictions, but nations at the core of the global economy, particularly those belonging to the OECD.[82] Within nations, there exist "unusual legal spaces, anomalous territories, and peculiar jurisdictions [...] city-states, havens, enclaves, free ports, high-tech parks, duty-free districts, and innovation hubs".[83] According to the Tax Justice Network of June 2025, and on the basis the Financial Secrecy Index (FSI), nations such as the US, Switzerland, Luxembourg, Germany, the Netherlands, and Ireland are widely recognized as among the world's leading enablers of financial secrecy.

As documented in the case of the US, one strategy used by corporate leaders to maximize shareholder value is through tax avoidance—thereby creating sustained demand for preferential tax regimes abroad.[84] The US has frequently played a dominant role in shaping this global tax landscape. It is estimated that US taxpayers hold approximately 4 trillion dollars in offshore accounts, with about 2 trillion dollars located in jurisdictions classified as tax havens. Moreover, despite the introduction of the *Foreign Account Tax Compliance Act*, US citizens can still exploit legal loopholes to conceal offshore assets. And despite multilateral efforts led by the OECD, the US—where wealth concentration ranks among the highest globally—does not participate fully in international information exchange, effectively behaving as a tax haven itself through strategic non-cooperation.[85] Only recently has some empirical evidence emerged—specifically within the European Union—suggesting that the public naming and shaming of tax havens may have tangible effects. For instance, it has been found that such reputational actions are associated with negative stock price reactions for firms with subsidiaries located in named tax haven jurisdictions.[86]

[81] On this specific topic, see Dharmapala (2023).
[82] Almost all European countries appear among the top 70 countries.
[83] Slobodian (2023, 2).
[84] Saez and Zucman (2019).
[85] De Simone and Stomberg (2023).
[86] Rusina (2020).

In the European Union, a notable concern is that the list of tax havens published in February 2025 includes only one of the world's twenty worst corporate tax havens as identified by the Tax Justice Network, just one of the fifteen worst corporate tax havens according to Oxfam's analysis,[87] and none of the ten jurisdictions that, according to the IMF, host more than 85% of all so-called phantom investments.[88] The EU's list appears highly selective and inadequate in addressing the broader issue of tax havens. Numerous examples of unaddressed practices can be found across Europe and are well documented in tax haven reports as well as in specialized academic and investigative studies.

It is important to recognize, however, that the concept of a tax haven is not universally defined, as there is no single, objective threshold that determines whether a country qualifies as one. In practice, any jurisdiction may function as a tax haven if it offers preferential treatment to individuals or corporations. According to *WorldData.info*, which compiles and compares several major international tax haven lists, approximately 75 jurisdictions worldwide may currently be classified as tax havens.[89] An analysis of these sources reveals that, among democratic countries, the US and Switzerland consistently rank at the top of the FSI, with Luxembourg, Germany, and the Netherlands also appearing in the top ten. According to the FSI 2025 report, the UK ranks as the 20th largest global contributor to financial secrecy. Also, a 2022 report by the Financial Times estimates that UK residents hold approximately 1.07 trillion dollars in untaxed offshore wealth; moreover, nearly 40% of global corporate investments are routed through tax havens via the UK. While fragmented, this evidence highlights the central role of financial secrecy in understanding the functionality of tax havens. Since users of tax havens are often non-residents with no legal ties to the jurisdiction, these jurisdictions are incentivized to maintain strict confidentiality in order to shield foreign wealth from detection by other governments and to avoid creating publicly accessible records. This practice makes it extremely difficult—if not impossible—to trace untaxed wealth.

[87] Oxfam (2016).

[88] Damgaard et al. (2019a).

[89] These lists include the "Corporate Tax Havens" list by Oxfam; the Financial Action Task Force black and grey lists; the EU list of non-cooperative jurisdictions; the IMF's blacklist of jurisdictions hosting phantom investments; the OECD's list of countries offering citizenship-by-investment; and the FSI, which assesses jurisdictions' potential for concealing wealth from foreign tax authorities.

It suggests that financial secrecy may, in fact, be a more decisive factor in global tax competition than the traditional race to the bottom in tax rates.

This complexity blurs the dichotomy between tax havens and non-tax havens. Countries not identified as tax havens in most classifications are nonetheless included in FSI.[90] Among others, Albania, Bosnia and Herzegovina, Canada, Cyprus, Ireland, Luxembourg, Malta, the Netherlands, Serbia, Switzerland, Turkey, and the US all appear in at least one of the main international lists. In this regard, it is striking that none of these countries are classified as tax havens in the European Union's official list. This raises fundamental concerns: within an integrated economic area such as the EU—where some member states are responsible for a significant share of global corporate tax abuse risks—maintaining such a narrow definition of tax havens, while simultaneously enforcing fiscal discipline that constrains public expenditure, including social spending, reveals how market democracy can be structured to benefit a select few.

Given the vast amounts of income and wealth that flow through tax havens, it is legitimate to ask how compensatory tax measures could operate effectively in a context where most economically advanced countries have abandoned the taxation of capital incomes and moved away from comprehensive tax models. A more uncomfortable yet essential question is whether compensatory taxes can truly be effective in the absence of financial capital controls and without international agreements aimed at regulating capital mobility. It is also worth noting that many of the countries identified as tax havens rank among the highest in the Freedom House index of political rights and civil liberties. For example, the major European countries functioning—at least partially—as tax havens have scores above 90 (out of 100), while the US scores 84. These are all consolidated democracies. Yet, despite their democratic credentials, they continue to offer preferential treatment to capital income, thereby contributing to rising inequality.

The importance of regulating speculative capital flows can also be inferred indirectly from trends in foreign direct investment (FDI). As recently argued, there is a close connection between FDI and international corporate tax avoidance.[91] While capital flows and stock holdings are not taxed, the returns they generate should be. A standard way to measure FDI significance is to examine the FDI-to-GDP ratio. Globally, this ratio

[90] Cobham et al. (2015).
[91] Lejour (2023).

increased from 36% in 2009 to 45% in 2017, before falling back to 40% in 2021. Financial centres such as Hong Kong, Ireland, Luxembourg, the Netherlands, Singapore, and Switzerland account for approximately 90% of FDI stocks located in tax havens. However, these countries represent less than 4.5% of global GDP, which implies that their FDI-to-GDP ratios exceed 500%—a clear indication that much of this investment is not related to productive activity, but rather driven by artificial financial arrangements.[92]

Furthermore, a substantial share of global FDI does not represent ultimate FDI but is instead rerouted through intermediary jurisdictions.[93] This implies that global FDI flows may increase as a result of greater reliance on conduit countries by multinational corporations, even in the absence of any corresponding rise in productive economic activity. These conduit countries often feature sophisticated legal and regulatory systems that cater to the needs of multinational enterprises,[94] which, in 2021 alone, invested approximately USD 40 trillion abroad. Only 14.6% of this was invested in the US, while the top five tax haven jurisdictions accounted for 44% of global FDI stocks. Asian economies have also become increasingly relevant, in part due to the tightening of anti-avoidance and anti-evasion rules in European countries. The distortions caused by conduit-based investment routes are starkly illustrated by the FDI stock-to-GDP ratios in certain jurisdictions: 26,754% in the British Virgin Islands; 18,440% in the Cayman Islands; 3,241% in Luxembourg; 1,271% in Cyprus; 350% in the Netherlands; 192% in Ireland; 174% in Switzerland; 121% in Belgium; and 93% in the UK.[95] As previously discussed, the UK, Luxembourg, and the Netherlands serve as central nodes in the global network of corporate tax planning,[96] functioning not necessarily to provide low statutory tax rates, but rather to enhance the investment climate and facilitate profit shifting across jurisdictions.

[92] Perhaps the most striking case is Luxembourg. According to official statistics, this country of 600,000 people hosts a stock of FDI of about USD 1.18 trillion, more than 14 times the country's GDP and more than India's GDP, which translates into FDI of USD 6.6 million per person. See Damgaard et al. (2019a).

[93] Unctad (2016) and Damgaard et al. (2019b).

[94] Mintz (2004); Takes et al. (2017).

[95] Data are from Lejour (2023).

[96] Van't Riet and Lejour (2018).

If there is one overarching lesson to be drawn from this overview, it is that no tax system can sustainably correct imbalances of such magnitude without a deliberate and coordinated political response. Yet, the persistent failure to act reflects the structural power of global economic elites—those who invest heavily in shaping favourable tax environments, maintaining opacity in financial regulation, and constraining the redistributive and regulatory capacities of the state. At the same time, these actors often promote the replacement of welfare state functions with market-based provision of public goods and services (health, education, etc.), intensifying both inequality and institutional erosion. Through this process of erosion, the fiscal contract is fragmented into a multitude of contracts, which benefit a few at the expense of many.

References

Acemoglu, D., Naidu, S., Restrepo, P., & Robinson, J. A. (2015). Democracy, redistribution, and inequality. In *Handbook of income distribution* (chapter 21). Elsevier.

Adam, S., & Miller, H. (2020). *The economics of a wealth tax.* Wealth Tax Commission Evidence Paper no. 3. The Wealth Tax Commission.

Ansell, B. W., & Samuels, D. J. (2018). *Why inequality does not undermine democracy.* Paper presented at the American Political Science Association (APSA) Annual Meeting. Available at https://wealthpol.web.ox.ac.uk/article/why-inequality-does-not-undermine-democracy. University of Oxford.

Arnold, S. (2014). Market democracy: Land of opportunity? *Critical Review, 26*(3–4), 239–258.

Audard, C. (2023). Addressing the rise of inequalities: How relevant is Rawls's critique of welfare state capitalism? *Journal of Social Philosophy, 55*(2), 221–237.

Bankman, J., & Shaviro, D. (2014). *Piketty in america: A tale of two literatures.* Stanford Law and Economics Olin Working Paper No. 469.

Bastani, S., & Waldenström, D. (2023). Taxing the wealthy: the choice between wealth and capital income taxation. *Oxford Review of Economic Policy, 39*, 604–616.

Bearer-Friend, J. (2021). Tax Without Cash. *Minnesota Law Review, 106*, 953–1016.

Bergolo, M., Londoño-Vélez, J., & Tortarolo, D. (2023). Tax progressivity and taxing the rich in developing countries: Lessons from Latin America. *Oxford Review of Economic Policy, 39*, 530–549.

Beveridge, W. (1942). *Social insurance and allied services* (Cmd. 6404). His Majesty's Stationery Office.

Brownlee, W. E. (2018). Tax Policy in the United States: Was there a "Neo-Liberal" revolution in the 1970s and 1980s? In G. Huerlimann, W. E. Brownlee, E. Ide (Eds.), *Worlds of taxation - The political economy of taxing, spending, and redistribution since 1945* (pp. 155–186). Palgrave MacMillan.
Buchanan, J. M., & Faith, R. A. (1989). Secession and the limits of taxation: Toward a theory of internal exit. *Journal of Theoretical Politics, 1*(1), 19–39.
Buchanan, J. M. (1994). Comportamento indotto dalle istituzioni nel mercato e in politica. *Notizie di Politeia, 10*(33–34), 4–19 (published in italian).
Cnossen, S. (2000). Taxing capital income in the nordic countries: A model for the European Union? In *Taxing capital income in the European Union - Issues and options for reform* (chapter 8). Oxford University Press.
Cobham, A., Jansky, P., & Meinzer, M. (2015). The financial secrecy index: Shedding new light on the geography of secrecy. *Economic Geography, 91*(3), 281–303.
Crouch, C. (2009). Privatised keynesianism: An unacknowledged policy regime. *The British Journal of Politics and International Relations, 11*, 382–399.
Damgaard, J., Elkjaer, T., & Johannesen, N. (2019a). The rise of phantom investments: Empty corporate shells in tax havens undermine tax collection. *IMF Finance and Development, 56*(3), 60.
Damgaard, J., Elkjaer, T., & Johannesen, N. (2019b). *What is real and what is not in the global FDI network?* IMF Working Paper 19/274.
Daunton, M. (2023). *The economic government of the world.* Penguin Random House.
De Simone, L., & Stomberg, B. (2023). Has FATCA succeeded in reducing tax evasion through foreign accounts? *Oxford Review of Economic Policy, 39*(3), 550–564.
Dharmapala, D. (2023). *Overview of the characteristics of tax havens.* Coase-Sandor Working Paper Series in Law and Economics No. 975. University of Chicago Law School.
Diamond, P., & Chwalisz, C. (2015). *The predistribution agenda: Tackling inequality and supporting sustainable growth.* I.B. Tauris and Co.
Economist Intelligence Unit. (2024). *Eiu's 2023 democracy index: Conflict and polarisation drive a new low for global democracy*, London.
Fessler, P., & Schürz, M. (2015). *Private wealth across European countries: The role of income, inheritance and the welfare state.* European Central Bank Working Paper Series, no. 1847.
Fleischer, M. P. (2017). Not so fast: The hidden difficulties of taxing wealth. In J. Knight, M. Schwartzberg (Eds.), *Wealth: NOMOS LVIII* (pp. 261–308). New York University Press.
Friedman, M. (1962). *Capitalism and freedom.* Chicago University Press.
Glantz, M., & Kissell, R. (2014). *Multi-asset risk modeling.* Elsevier.

Gordon, D. M. (1972). Taxation of the poor and the normative theory of tax incidence. *American Economic Review, 57*, 731–758.
Gründler, K., & Krieger, T. (2021). Using machine learning for measuring democracy: A practitioners guide and a new updated dataset for 186 countries from 1919 to 2019. *European Journal of Political Economy, 70*(1), 102047.
Güçeri, I., & Slemrod, J. (2023). Taxing the rich (more). *Oxford Review of Economic Policy, 39*, 399–405.
Hall, P. A., & Soskice, D. (eds.) (2001). *Varieties of capitalism. The institutional foundation of comparative advantage*. Oxford University Press.
Hayek, F. A. (1944). *The road to serfdom*. Routledge.
Kaufmann, F., & Nullmeier, F. (2021). Post-war welfare state development: The 'Golden Age'. In D. Béland, K. Morgan, H. Obinger, C. Pierson (Eds.), *The Oxford handbook of the welfare state* (chapter 6). Oxford University Press.
Kellee, S. T. (2007). *Capitalism without democracy: The private sector in contemporary China*. Cornell University Press.
Keynes, J. M. (1936). *The general theory of employment, interest and money*. MacMillan.
Krieger, T. (2022). *Measuring democracy*. ZEW Discussion Paper, 22-063.
Kopczuk, W. (2023). The messy boundary between pass-through and corporate taxation. *Oxford Review of Economic Policy, 39*(3), 451–459.
Lauth, H., & Schlenkrich, O. (2020). Making trade-offs visible: Theoretical and methodological considerations about the relationship between dimensions and institutions of democracy and empirical findings. *Politics and Governance, 6*(1), 78–91.
Lazonick, W. (2014). Profits without prosperity: Stock buybacks manipulate the market and leave most Americans worse off. *Harvard Business Review, 92*(9), 46–55.
Lejour, A. (2023). *Good tax practices in the fight against tax avoidance: The signalling role of FDI data*. European Parliament, Policy Department for Economic, Scientific and Quality of Life Policies.
Matzner, E., & Streeck, W. (1991). *Beyond keynesianism: The socio-economics of production and full employment*. Edward Elgar Publishing.
Merkel, W. (2014). Is capitalism compatible with democracy? *Zeitschrift fur Vergleichende Politikwissenschaft, 8*, 109–128.
Mintz, J. (2004). Conduit entities: Implications of indirect tax-efficient financing structures for real investments. *International Tax and Public Finance, 114*(4), 419–434.
Munck, G. L., & Verkuilen, J. (2002). Conceptualizing and meassuring democracy: Evaluating alternative indices. *Comparative Political Studies, 35*(1),5–34.
Murphy, L., & Nagel, T. (2002). *The myth of ownership: Taxes and justice*. Oxford University Press.

Naidu, S. (2017). A Political economy take on W/Y. In H. Boushey, J. B. DeLong, M. Steinbaum (Eds.), *After Piketty: The agenda for economics and inequality* (chapter 5). Harvard University Press.

O'Connell, M., & Ward, A. (2020). Shareholder theory/shareholder value. In S. Idowu, N. Schmidpeter, N. Capaldi, L. Zu, M. Del Baldo, R. Abreu (Eds.), *Encyclopedia of sustainable management* (chapter 49). Springer Nature.

O'Neill M. (2020). Power, predistribution, and social justice. *Philosophy, 95*, 63–91.

OECD. (2009). *Growing unequal? Income distribution and poverty in OECD countries.* OECD Publishing.

OECD. (2015). *Economic policy reforms 2015: Going for growth.* OECD Publishing.

Oxfam. (2016). *Tax battles - the dangerous global race to the bottom on corporate tax.* Oxfam Policy Paper. Oxfam International. Available at https://www.oxfam.org/en/research/tax-battles-dangerous-global-race-bottom-corporate-tax.

Perret, S. (2021). Why were most wealth taxes abandoned and is this time different? *Fiscal Studies, 42*, 539–563.

Piketty, T. (2013). *Capital in the twenty-first century.* Harvard University Press.

Piketty, T., & Saez, E. (2013). Top incomes and the Great Recession: Recent evolutions and policy implications. *IMF Economic Review, 61*(3), 456–478.

Positive Money. (2022). *The power of big finance - How to reclaim our democracy from the banking lobby*, London.

Ramos Pinto, P. (2019). Inequality by numbers: The making of a global political issue. In C. O. Christiansen, S. B. Jensen (Eds.), *Histories of global inequality.* Springer International Publishing.

Reich, R. B. (2015). *Saving capitalism: for the many, not the few.* Knopf A.

Rousseau, J. J. [1755] (1999). *Discourse on political economy and the social contract.* Oxford University Press.

Rusina, A. (2020). Name and shame? Evidence from the European Union tax haven blacklist. *International Tax and Public Finance, 27*, 1364–1424.

Saez, E., & Zucman, G. (2019). *The triumph of injustice - How the rich dodge taxes and how to make them pay.* W.W. Norton and Company.

Sawyer, M. (2024). *Financialization - Economic and social impacts.* Agenda Publishing.

Scheve, K., & Stavasage, D. (2016). *Taxing the rich - A history of fiscal fairness in the United States and Europe.* Princeton University Press.

Simons, H. C. (1938). *Personal income taxation - The definition of income as a problem of fiscal policy.* University of Chicago Press.

Sirowy, L., & Inkeles, A. (1990). The effects of democracy on economic growth and inequality: A review. *Studies in Comparative International Development, 25*(1), 126–157.

Slemrod, J., & Chen X. (2023). Are capital gains the Achilles' heel of taxing the rich? *Oxford Review of Economic Policy, 39*(3), 438–451.

Slobodian, Q. (2023). *Crack-up capitalism. Market radicals and the dream of a world without democracy.* MacMillan, Penguin Random House.

Sørensen, P. B. (1994). From the global income tax to the dual income tax: Recent tax reforms in the nordic countries. *International Tax and Public Finance, 1*, 57–80.

Sørensen, P. B. (2005). Dual income taxation: Why and how? *FinanzArchiv/Public Finance Analysis, 61*(4), 559–586.

Stiglitz, J. E. (2013). *The price of inequality: How today's divided society endangers our future.* Norton and Co. Inc.

Streeck, W. (2016). How will capitalism end? *New Left Review, 87*, 35–64.

Takes, J. W., Heemskerk, E. M., Garcia-Bernardo, J., & Fichtner, F. (2017). Uncovering offshore financial centers: Conduits and sinks in the global corporate ownership network. *Scientific Report, 7*, 1–10.

Tomasi, J. (2012). *Free market fairness.* Princeton University Press.

Unctad. (2016). *World investment report 2024.* United Nations Publications.

Van't Riet, M., & Lejour, A. (2018). Optimal tax routing: Network analysis of FDI diversion. *International Tax and Public Finance, 25*(5), 1321–1371.

Volpi, A. (2024). *I Padroni del Mondo.* Laterza.

Weale, A. (2013). The property-owning democracy versus the welfare state. *Analyse and Kritik, 1*, 37–54.

Winters, J. A. (2011). *Oligarchy.* Cambridge University Press.

Winters, J. A., & Page, B. I. (2009). Oligarchy in the United States? *Perspectives on Politics, 7*(4), 731–751.

Wolf, M., Haar, K., & Hoedeman, O. (2014). *The fire power of the financial lobby: A survey of the size of the financial lobby at the EU level.* Joint Report published by Corporate Europe Observatory (CEO), Austrian Federal Chamber of Labor (Arbeiterkammer), and the Austrian Trade Union Federation (OGB). April. Online available at: http://corporateeurope.org/sites/default/files/attachments/financial_lobby_report.pdf

Zuboff, S. (2019). *The age of surveillance capitalism - The fight for a human future at the new frontier of power.* Public Affairs.

CHAPTER 4

Building the Fiscal Contract in a Democratic Welfare State

Abstract We present a novel argument in support of Rawls's property-owning democracy by articulating a fiscal contract embedded within the broader framework of the social contract. Justice in both the distribution of the benefits generated by society's background institutions and the allocation of the tax burden depends on the validity of the reciprocity principle, as upheld by the fiscal contract. We propose the development of a Democratic Welfare State model as a pragmatic approximation of property-owning democracy. The Democratic Welfare State establishes a set of minimum institutional requirements designed to counteract the effects of market-captured democracy: restoring a comprehensive income tax; reaffirming the link between taxation and public spending; complementing the ability-to-pay principle with a renewed focus on the benefit principle; eliminating unjustified preferential tax treatments; ensuring universal access to core welfare programmes; defining the conditions under which a basic income or minimum wage could be implemented; and rethinking the international dimension of the social contract.

Keywords Fiscal democracy • Property-owning democracy • Democratic welfare state • Health • Education and labour market • Fragmented society

P. Liberati, M. Paradiso, *Rebuilding Fiscal Democracy*,
https://doi.org/10.1057/978-3-032-04859-2_4

Distributive Justice and Taxation

As we have argued in the preceding chapters, in market democracies the rhetoric of tax justice has concealed the dissolution of the fiscal contract and of the objectives of distributive justice, which have been effectively absorbed into the outcomes of allocative justice as realized through the market. When, by contrast, the assessment of distributive justice is framed within a contractualist perspective, no limits are imposed on the role of the state beyond those implied by the system of reciprocal relationships among individuals—that is, the structure of rights and duties regulating the interactions among cooperating individuals engaged in the production of public goods and services. By tying taxation to public spending, it becomes possible to establish an implicit upper bound on tax revenue collection—namely, a level that should not exceed (but should be consistent with) the financing of the basic social and economic institutions envisaged in the social contract. Thus, while the connection between taxes and corresponding benefits cannot imply a direct one-to-one correspondence, it can be interpreted as a more abstract—but no less concrete—relationship between taxation and the benefits of social cooperation in the production of public goods. From the taxpayer's perspective, the link between the amount of taxes paid and the quality of public services received remains tangible. The taxpayer is more likely to view the tax obligation as justified when they perceive a meaningful outcome stemming from it; conversely, they are naturally inclined to resist the obligation when they fail to recognize the benefits of compliance. A fiscal contract would, in principle, help prevent this disaffection with taxation.

Once progressivity is understood as a method of applying the ability to pay principle in connection with the benefits of public expenditure, equality of opportunity is ensured through the universal provision of public goods. This approach does not subordinate access to public goods to any prior fulfilment of tax obligations by individual citizens. The connection between taxation and public spending is of fundamental importance and motivates the taxpayer's reaction when this relationship is violated. Also the current "restlessness and unhappiness of many voters has, at its root, a disjunction between the different elements of the tax state"—a disjunction that is also believed to drive significant voter mobilization, rooted in "the disjunction between the quality of services voters want, and their willingness to pay for them through taxes", thereby undermining the very foundations of any social contract.[1] The predominance of the ability to pay principle over the benefit principle in both theoretical discourse and tax system design has reinforced the ethical assumption of an individual's right to pre-tax income as if such income could be generated by the market independently of any public intervention. As a result, vertical equity has increasingly prevailed over horizontal equity, producing a narrow and partial interpretation of the tax justice dilemma. This has contributed to the development and consolidation of tax systems that conflict with the democratic principles of cooperation and reciprocity and are ultimately inadequate to ensure the stable provision of public goods and services.

This conceptual framework has important implications for the structure of taxation. First, it is imperative to avoid any under-provision of public goods and services that the social contract defines as universal and essential to the realization of equality of opportunity. Second, taxes should be as broadly based as possible; a distorted distribution of tax burdens would violate the principle of horizontal equity and weaken the link between taxes paid and the benefits of public spending. Third, and consequently, the fiscal contract should reject both the predominance of redistribution over the financing function of taxation, and the influence of market mechanisms in shaping tax design—particularly when they lead to preferential treatment, exemptions, or fragmentation of tax bases according to income source. The general character of taxation is essential to the integrity of a fiscal contract, as it restores to progressivity the role of a differential price to be paid for the provision of public goods—a differential price that can be justified through the adoption of the ability to pay principle, provided that this principle is understood in relation to the benefits of public spending. Contrary to alternative interpretations of progressivity,[2] this is the only approach that meaningfully reclaims the predistributive function of reducing inequality—a function that is distinct from, and more realistic than, the normative aims of optimal taxation theory or the elusive goal of influencing the behaviour of high-income earners through tax policy.

This conception of taxation directly challenges the notion that economic analysis has little to contribute to value judgments, or that questions of distribution lie solely within the domain of ethics or political ideology. When taxes are understood as the contribution paid for public goods, the

[1] Gamble (2015, 25).
[2] See Barnes (2015).

questions of how much to tax and how to distribute tax burdens become economic problems—particularly in light of the fact that many public goods generate indivisible benefits or are provided free of charge. This framework also addresses a longstanding dilemma: whether progressivity can only be justified by an inherent objection to social inequality—as exemplified by Henry Simons, who defended progressive taxation on the grounds that inequality was inherently unlovely.[3] The reframing of progressive taxation—as a form of benefit taxation grounded in the ability to pay—would shift the focus away from a narrowly redistributive role and toward taxation's broader function as a safeguard of a stable social contract. Consequently, there would be no compelling reason to tax extreme wealth through exceptional or special tax instruments. As argued, all income-generating activities depend not solely on individual effort but also on a wide array of public goods and services—such as the rule of law, the protection of property rights, infrastructure, education, healthcare, and other tangible and institutional supports provided by the state.[4] In fulfilling this role, the tax system—is far from serving as a mere compensatory mechanism for the absence of public rules aimed at preventing the concentration of wealth and income in the primary distribution. At the same time, this model of taxation is not primarily designed with the aim of relying on targeted and means-tested monetary transfers to compensate for an inadequate provision of public goods and services. This is not to suggest that monetary transfers should be entirely avoided; they may still be necessary to alleviate poverty. However, their function should not be extended to the point of replacing the direct and universal provision of public goods and services.

The relationship between public spending and taxation, between ends and means, within the fiscal contract thus yields essential guidelines for ensuring that the design of the tax system is consistent with the process of distributive justice, which, in the cooperative democracy, operates autonomously from the logic of allocative justice pursued through the market. The contrast between the contractual conception of distributive justice and the economic notion of allocative justice carries important implications for the definition of fiscal citizenship. In the first case, individuals mutually recognize one another's right to a fair share of public goods as the outcome

[3] Simons (1938); Blum and Kalven (1953); Avi-Yonah (2002).

[4] Graetz (1997).

of collective cooperation. Accordingly, the notion of fiscal citizenship, as defined by the fiscal contract, is grounded in the link between individual's right to a share of public goods and their duty to contribute through taxation. In the second case, by contrast, the individual is viewed merely as an agent with preferences over the allocation of available resources. Within this framework, no explicit connection exists between the taxes one pays and the public benefits one receives.

Justice and Taxation in the Rawlsian Property-Owning Democracy

The rhetoric of tax justice has recently drawn upon Rawls's concept of fairness, reducing it to a vaguely ethical notion that significantly distorts its original meaning. Saez and Zucman[5] have argued that tax systems should be designed to benefit the least advantaged members of society, echoing Rawls's Difference Principle.[6] Their advocacy for a wealth tax is framed not as a call for absolute equality, but as a way to ensure that inequality remains justifiable and socially legitimate. This interpretation of Rawls's theory in the context of taxation, especially wealth taxation, is, at best, incomplete and potentially misleading.[7]

This misinterpretation largely stems from an attempt to situate Rawls within a utilitarian framework. In fact, Rawls regards aggregate utility as an elusive concept fraught with indeterminacy, vagueness, and ambiguity.[8] His theory fundamentally comprises two principles of justice: first, each individual possesses an indefeasible claim to an adequate scheme of equal basic liberties—a principle often overlooked; second, social and economic inequalities must satisfy two conditions: (a) they must be linked to offices and positions accessible to all under conditions of fair equality of opportunity; and (b) they must be arranged so as to benefit the least advantaged members of society—the difference principle.

[5] See, for example, Saez and Zucman (2019, 130). Rawls's theory of justice has even been imported into the field of optimal taxation theory. For a discussion, see Walraevens (2023).

[6] Rawls (1999).

[7] It is important to acknowledge that the imperative to tax the wealthy emerges subsequent to several decades during which neoliberalism aimed "to scale back welfare states to a social minimum, a residual welfare state, where spending was targeted primarily on need, and universalism rejected" Gamble (2015, 24).

[8] Rawls (2001); Freeman (2007).

Within economic literature, the difference principle is frequently cited as justification for pro-poor taxation policies. Nonetheless, this emphasis neglects that Rawls conceives the underlying economic system—and consequently the operational meaning of the difference principle—as one in which "all citizens should be placed in a position where they can interact with one another from a position of independence and equality rather than their being the recipients of transfers determined by a political elite exercising political and economic control".[9] Therefore, a full realization of Rawls's model of distributive justice does not readily translate into simply imposing taxes on extreme wealth.

According to Rawls, the proper implementation of the difference principle depends on the realization of the first principle, which is a fully adequate scheme of equal basic liberties. In its absence, the use of the second principle might not be appropriate. This means that taxing the rich and redistributing to the poor will not be decisive for the realization of the Rawlsian model without a prior balance of power between the state and the market. This explains why Rawls writes that "to see the full force of the difference principle, it should be taken in the context of a property-owning democracy [...] it is a principle of reciprocity, or mutuality, for society seen as a fair system of cooperation among free and equal citizens from one generation to the next".[10] In market democracies, however, the difference principle is instead interpreted as a means of alleviating the worst-off or as a principle of benevolence to safeguard the functioning of the market[11] and to preserve the proliferation of inequality.

Indeed, for Rawls, the concept of distributive justice extends beyond the mere concept of tax justice. It involves choosing a social system[12] and is not solely a matter of taxing extreme wealth. The most significant distributive effects originate from the principles of a social contract defined *ex ante*, as embodied in the concept of property-owning democracy (POD).[13] To the extent that the 'tax the rich' argument fails to consider the principles of cooperation and reciprocity in democratic functioning, a wealth tax may prove ineffective in securing social rights. This is not to say that Rawls does not consider taxes. Rather, in Rawls's view, highly progressive

[9] Weale (2013, 38).
[10] Rawls (1999, xv).
[11] Fernandez Manzano (2022, 92).
[12] Freeman (2018).
[13] Rawls (2001), especially part IV.

taxes and inheritance and gift taxes are essential tools for preventing the intergenerational accumulation of wealth. However, if left alone, they are unable to counteract the accumulation of power, or prevent a small part of society from controlling the economy and political life.[14] All these measures should encourage a permanent, widespread, and far more equal dispersion of real property and productive assets. In this sense, Rawls does not rely solely on a system of monetary transfers to the poor or means-tested welfare provisions, even though these have formed part of his policy agenda. They could be part of a wider programme in which the government guarantees a social minimum "by such devices as a graded income supplement (a so-called negative income tax)" after having guaranteed liberty of equal citizenship, conscience, and freedom, as well as equality of opportunity.[15]

Rawls is also often understood as providing the theoretical basis for the traditional welfare state to redistribute resources, which, as recently argued, would justify using tax and transfer systems to benefit the least well-off.[16] However, he did not believe that the traditional welfare state could fully realize the principle of justice.[17] In Rawls's view, questions of justice cannot be resolved through piecemeal political reforms; rather, they require a global institutional arrangement based on governments engaging in planning, regulation, and ruling the market, as well as providing essential and non-essential public goods. This institutional arrangement must therefore ensure that each new generation has the same equal opportunities and life chances.[18] In this context, the aim is not to maximize economic growth (or utility, as in the framework of economics), but rather to prevent any group from dominating economic life.[19] Thus, attention is paid not to the consequences of capitalism (*ex post* focus), but to the foundational institutions of a market economy (*ex ante* focus). This implies that, as it is traditionally understood, capitalism may hinder the development of a well-functioning democracy due to its tendency to reduce the scope of politics in favour of the market.[20]

[14] Rawls (2001, 160–162); Schefczyk (2013).
[15] Rawls (1999, 243). See also Forrester (2019), especially chapter 4.
[16] Saez and Zucman (2019).
[17] O'Neill and Williamson (2012).
[18] Weale (2013).
[19] O'Neill and Williamson (2012, 4).
[20] Fernandez Manzano (2022, 92).

While the notion of POD may be dismissed as utopian, it is nevertheless possible to envision a feasible approximation under specific institutional conditions. The Rawlsian idea was, to some extent, deeply inspired by an important book by James Meade, in which a compelling account of how institutions tasked with creating a more egalitarian economy should treat wealth was presented.[21] An interesting feature of Meade's contribution is that he was more radical than Rawls in suggesting that a property-owning democracy would require 'capital predistribution' more than 'labour predistribution' or trade union capitalism.[22] This would involve expanding public ownership of capital; this expansion would be achieved through a combination of private means and a socialist state that would increase public ownership of capital via something akin to a citizen trust. Indeed, according to Meade "extreme inequalities in the ownership of property are [...] undesirable, quite apart from any inequalities of income which they may imply. A man with much property has great bargaining strength, as well as a great sense of security, independence, and freedom; and he enjoys these things not only vis-à-vis his propertyless fellow citizens, but also vis-à-vis the public authorities. He can snap his fingers at those on whom he must rely for an income; for he can always live for a time on his capital. The propertyless man must continuously and without interruption acquire his income by working for an employer or by qualifying to receive it from a public authority. An unequal distribution of property means an unequal distribution of power and status even if it is prevented from causing too unequal a distribution of income".[23]

Interpreted as social models to limit the unequal distribution of power in society, Meade's social liberalism and Rawls's POD are perhaps no less utopian proposals than worldwide wealth taxes.[24] Over the past 40 years, democracies have arguably allowed markets to operate without rules, or with weak formal rules particularly in relation to the concentration

[21] Meade (1964).

[22] See O'Neill (2020). Edmundson (2017) has convincingly provided an interpretation of Rawls (2001), specifying the common ground between property-owning democracy and liberal democratic socialism, as well as the critique of the capitalist regime. In a different vein, Thomas (2016) maintains the "uniqueness thesis", arguing that property-owning democracy is the only institutional model that fully embodies the core values of liberal republicanism—such as non-domination, civic equality, and economic independence.

[23] Meade (1964, 38–39).

[24] As, for example, in Piketty et al. (2014).

of economic and political power. Once the market is allowed to gain this power, democracies may weaken, giving rise to the oligarchization of society. Free and deregulated markets may have contributed to the decline of embedded democracies worldwide, including the functioning and confidence of mature democracies.[25] The oligarchization of society has gone hand in hand with the dissolution of the social contract in market democracies, where democracy has ended up serving the market, relegating the state to the role of a mercantilist court designed to protect the market's elites. Consequently, the invisible hand of the market has prevailed over the visible hand of democracy, as well as over the principles of distributive justice that express the democratic conception of society as a system of cooperation and reciprocity among equal individuals. Since the social contract is a collective agreement, in which institutions representing the basic structure of society are designed to benefit everyone on the basis of reciprocity, a complex system of principles and rules embodied in the political constitution is needed. In the economic sphere, the social contract must explicitly state whether the common goal of economic activity is, for example, the fair distribution of the national product between workers and firms—especially for what concerns the distribution of bargaining power—how the common rules for achieving this goal are set, and which political and social authorities are responsible for achieving it. As noted above, limiting public policies—including tax policies—to the role of compensatory measures is insufficient for a stable long-term solution. This is because the degree of compensation may become arbitrary, and the redistribution process itself may be undermined by the political and economic power of the richest part of the population.

Obviously, the existence of a social contract does not guarantee that it will not be violated; a social contract can be reneged on by either party after its stipulation. Actual laws may attempt to circumvent the constitutional framework, or individuals may react to failures of the social contract by violating the principles of mutuality and reciprocity. In both cases, this would imply that the social contract is no longer unanimously agreed upon. In this context, is the recent growth in inequality the outcome of a social contract that is no longer shared by everyone? Or, to add another recent debate, is the environmental movement a sign that the social contract

[25] A detailed treatment of this democratic recession is given in Diamond (2015) and in Wolf (2023).

of maximizing profits irrespective of environmental consequences should be updated to take into account new arguments that were previously underrated? These questions cannot be ignored on the basis that "the market requires it", leaving compensatory tax measures to correct the market's most undesirable outcomes. The idea that markets are impersonal forces should indeed be rejected, as they are in fact the outcome of the prevailing interests of capital owners over those of other stakeholders.

The key issue is identifying an architecture for an economic constitution that can realize the principles of cooperation and mutuality. In the Rawlsian social contract, rules only comply with the principle of justice if they are chosen in the original position, a position in which no person knows what their place in society will be (the Rawlsian veil of ignorance). This concept is particularly relevant in the current context of growing inequality, as the aim of POD is "to disperse the ownership of wealth and capital, and thus to prevent a small part of society from controlling the economy, and indirectly, political life as well".[26] This explains why higher taxes to reduce inequalities and the concentration of income and wealth would appear as a failure from a Rawlsian perspective, since in a POD such a concentration would be prevented from occurring. However, regardless of efforts to apply taxes to extreme wealth, the outcome of these compensatory measures will never be consistent with the structure of a POD. The fact that they mimic the Rawlsian difference principle does not make them legitimate in the context of a Rawlsian conception of democracy.

Rawls is clear on this topic: POD does not require redistribution *ex post*, but widespread ownership *ex ante*. The manner in which this widespread ownership is to be achieved is open to debate, including its inclusion in either a private or social system of property ownership.[27] As some have observed, Rawls is not enthusiastic about using taxes and transfers to address income inequality.[28] The reason is that, by making property holdings more dispersed, the need for taxes and transfers would be significantly reduced. Emphasizing the difference principle while neglecting the context in which it develops provides only a partial interpretation of Rawls's theory.

[26] Rawls (2001, 139).
[27] Clark and Gintis (1978); Krouse and McPherson (1988).
[28] Krouse and McPherson (1988).

Without the background of POD, the difference principle is indeed powerless to find permanent solutions to the concentration of economic resources. It is also erroneously employed by its misinterpreters to justify tax and transfer systems in the context of traditional welfare state capitalism. If the market generates a highly unequal distribution of income and wealth, the Rawlsian characterization of the difference principle cannot be invoked if growing inequality results from equal liberty and fair opportunity being violated *ex ante*. Thus, for the difference principle to work properly, it must be placed in the context of equality of the underlying distribution of property and opportunities, in a kind of lexicographic order.[29] In fact, POD requires more than a standard tax/transfer system; it requires that all individuals should be able to engage with one another on an equal and independent footing, rather than relying on resources allocated by a political elite that holds power over both politics and the economy.[30] Whatever the route, there is no doubt that cooperation, mutuality, and reciprocity are milestones of the Rawlsian social contract.

In this framework, social justice defines the institutional arrangements that enable each individual to contribute fully to social well-being. This perspective has attracted substantial criticism—in particular, the argument that a capitalist system could never generate "the very considerable political power [...] to enforce the sorts of wage rates, tax policies, transfer payments, and job regulation called for by the difference principle",[31] and that applying the difference principle within such a system would demand unsustainable levels of commitment to realize its redistributive aims.[32] This also helps explain why public economics adopted the Rawlsian theory only insofar as it expanded the formal representation of a social welfare function—but advanced no further. This criticism stems from the belief that there is only one model of capitalism (neoliberal) and one model of democracy (market democracy). To be clear, POD (and Rawls) does not reject capitalism; rather, it emphasizes the alternative strategy of creating institutions "that will ensure a more equal underlying distribution of physical and human capital, or property and skill endowments, so that *the market will generate less unequal results to begin with*".[33] However, this

[29] Rawls (2001, 42–44).
[30] Weale (2013).
[31] Wolff (1977, 202).
[32] Clark and Gintis (1978).
[33] Krouse and McPherson (1988, 90); emphasis ours.

implies a system of common goals and rules that rejects the development of undue concentrations of economic and political power. In POD, the rationale for controlling political and economic inequalities is to prevent one part of society from dominating the rest. When these two forms of inequality become substantial, they tend to reinforce one another, enabling a privileged few—through their control of the political process—to establish a legal and property system that secures their dominant position. This enables them to decide what is produced, control working conditions and the terms of employment offered, and shape the direction and volume of real savings and investment, as well as the pace of innovation. All of these factors determine what society becomes over time.[34]

To this end, a just social contract requires a constitutional phase in which common goals are shared, as well as procedures for creating and applying laws that satisfy constitutional aims.[35] To ensure that this process aligns with the actual functioning of contemporary economic systems, and assuming that the market is chosen as the foundation of the economic order, a constitutional phase involving all citizens should determine the limits of what the market can and cannot do. According to Rawls, no constitution can be considered just unless it embodies democratic principles and provides citizens with equal basic liberties and rights to political participation. The fair value of political liberties places a constraint on distributive inequality as it ensures that citizens "have roughly the same chance of attaining positions of political authority irrespective of their economic and social class".[36] Thus, the fair value of political liberties introduces a constraint on distributive inequality before the difference principle applies: "[t]hese liberties include those of liberty of conscience and freedom of thought, liberty of the person, and equal political rights. The political system, which I assume to be some form of constitutional democracy, would not be a just procedure if it did not embody these liberties".[37]

[34] Rawls (2001, 130–131).

[35] For a discussion of the constitutional phase, see Michelman (2003), Freeman (2007), Edmundson (2017, 65–76).

[36] Rawls (1999, 197). See also Rawls (2001, 46)

[37] Rawls (1999, 173).

From Market Democracy to Cooperative Democracy: The Democratic Welfare State

The central idea of our approach lies in approximating the model of POD, drawing from it the essential element of pre-distributive intervention to secure the conditions for the existence of a society as a fair system of reciprocity and cooperation. These are the defining features of a cooperative democracy, in which the benefits generated by the basic institutions and the distribution of the tax burden depend on the validity of the reciprocity principle, as upheld by the fiscal contract.[38]

Hereafter, we will refer to predistribution as a set of policies intended to transcend the traditional neoliberal capitalist paradigm[39] and to reshape the relationship between the market and the state. These policies aim to address the economic void created by the decline of the Beveridge-Keynes model of full employment and the welfare state. Since in a market democracy, redistribution can only dampen, rather than smooth out, higher inequality in the primary distribution of income,[40] what is proposed here is a concept of predistribution that does not seek to compensate losers, but rather to reshape the functioning of markets to reduce the need for compensation. In this vein, the focus should be on market outcomes that encourage a more equal distribution of economic power and rewards before governments collect taxes or pay benefits, in order to establish a more egalitarian approach than traditional redistributive tools can do.[41]

Even after accepting criticisms about the blurred temporal distinction between *ex ante* and *ex post*,[42] this distinction could be maintained to clarify the subtle difference between what governments can control before the market's economic actions take place and what they must do after

[38] Thomas (2016) has argued that POD deploys a comprehensive set of liberal institutional tools to counter inequality, including public services, progressive taxation, and equal access to productive assets. He supports a form of (theoretical) predistribution inspired by John Roemer's coupon socialism (Roemer, 1994), which guarantees each citizen an equal, non-transferable share in the ownership of the means of production, while preserving the efficiency of the market. This model aims to prevent the concentration of wealth and power, promote intergenerational fairness, and ensure that economic institutions uphold the principles of justice as fairness.

[39] Tsarouhas (2015).

[40] Gregg (2015, 81).

[41] Hacker (2011); Petroni (2015).

[42] O'Neill (2020).

these actions have occurred. Since the outcome of the market may differ depending on how it is regulated, different *afters* may result from different *befores*. Although the possibility that predistribution and redistribution may be complementary tools is not rejected, the hypothesis that a pre-distribution pillar could consist of increases in top marginal tax rates able to drive down both net and gross pre-tax levels of top pay is hardly consistent with this approach.[43] While some authors regard this possible effect as an example of a typical predistributive measure,[44] it is worth noting that the effect itself is entirely driven by individual preferences and thus remains outside the scope of a social contract. Economic regimes in which selective contracts emerge—depending on the relative power of different groups—and which may exert coercive effects on other segments of the population that do not share the same information should be rejected. In such cases, the principles of mutuality and reciprocity, rather than being universally applied, become selective, with the corresponding benefits being distributed only to potentially small segments of society. This fragmentation of the social contract could have profound implications for the functioning of democracy, leading to a society in which certain individuals possess sufficient power to influence political decisions.

From this perspective, Rawls argues that the welfare state is not an effective system for achieving his vision of democracy. He contends that welfare state capitalism does not dismantle the concentration of capital in private hands, nor does it prevent the wealthy from exerting greater influence over the political process, thereby undermining the possibility of implementing sufficiently substantial tax and transfer policies to effectively address inequalities. Moreover, the welfare state creates a divide between those who primarily depend on government for their income and those who derive resources from the market.[45] Rawls asserts that, although basic needs could be satisfied *ex post* by welfare state provisions, the issue of social justice remains unresolved if the principles of reciprocity and cooperation are not applied *ex ante* to prevent inequalities. In this sense, the redistributive mechanisms of the welfare state may, in fact, serve to legitimize society's dependence on market democracy.

[43] We refer to the Piketty-Saez-Stantcheva effect. See Piketty et al. (2014).

[44] O'Neill (2020, 83).

[45] Rawls (2001); O'Neill and Williamson (2012, 3).

Rawls's critique of the welfare state's failure to embody a principle of reciprocity is pivotal for understanding the superiority of the POD model. He argues that the welfare state is compatible with significant inequalities in the distribution of property and economic control, which leads to the concentration of political power in a few hands.[46] Furthermore, the welfare state does not adequately recognize the fair value of political liberties; it often provides social benefits based on need, a practice that may undermine democratic citizenship by perpetuating long-term financial insecurity and social dependency, especially among those who do not own capital or inherit wealth.[47] Moreover, the welfare state can foster the creation of an underclass—people who are dependent on welfare, disillusioned with public political participation, and disengaged from the broader political culture. According to Rawls, the foundational principles of such a model of Welfare State Capitalism (WSC) are not rooted in respect for individuals as equals, but in notions of charity and compassion, which may ultimately lead to stigmatization.[48] This mirrors the US model of residual welfare characterized by limited coverage, widespread means-testing, and pronounced social stratification, all of which fall short of realizing the property-owning democracy.[49] It follows that WSC could be interpreted as a need-based system, in contrast to a rights-based welfare system, wherein high-quality services are universally accessible to all citizens, and all citizens actively participate in the process of defining their common institutional challenges.[50] Furthermore, equality of opportunity would necessitate both unbiased selection for social positions and the provision of essential resources to allow talented individuals to fully develop their potential.[51]

It is important to note that the reasons why Rawls critiques the welfare state align with the reasons why public economics often supports it. For Rawls, insurance against accidents and misfortunes cannot form the

[46] See also Weale (2013).

[47] Petroni (2015).

[48] Rawls (2001, 135–140).

[49] In Esping-Andersen's (1990) typology, this model is classified as a liberal welfare system, characterized by its limited scope in comparison to the Nordic and Continental models, as well as the later Southern European model. See also the discussion in Castles and Mitchell (1992).

[50] Rothstein (1998).

[51] Scanlon (2018).

foundation of a fair social contract. In the case of the welfare state, it also fails to establish the 'decent minimum' below which no individual should fall, as the concept of society within POD is fundamentally one of cooperation. Indeed, Rawls contends that WSC has proven inadequate in preventing growing inequalities, even in Western countries where welfare states are more developed. As argued, WSC leads to vast inequalities in wealth, "which are typically accompanied by gross inequalities in political power and educational and professional opportunities",[52] thus leaving the interests of the middle and lower classes politically under-represented.[53] In contrast, public economics, with its focus on market failures, emphasizes the insurance principle on which a welfare state should ideally be based.

Nevertheless, one possible way to reconcile the tension between WSC and POD is through the concept of a Democratic Welfare State (DWS), understood as a functional set of tools designed to facilitate the realization of a cooperative democracy. A valuable starting point is Freeman's analysis of the economic institutions within a POD, particularly his comparison between POD and WSC.[54] In addition, recent proposals aimed at approximating POD have also been incorporated, such as the concept of the realistically utopian welfare state (RUWS).[55] We propose that the structure of a DWS should be grounded in the concept of predistribution, which can be defined as a set of market reforms aimed at encouraging a "more equal distribution of economic power and rewards before governments collect taxes and pays out benefits".[56] Even in light of some critiques, which rightfully points out that 'before' and 'after' may create conceptual ambiguities, we maintain that the concept of predistribution is consistent with Rawls' emphasis on ensuring equality *ex ante* rather than *ex post*.[57] Rawls recognized as fundamental to the definition of POD the moment—or period—in which the implementation of the social contract intervenes in the processes of wealth accumulation: "property-owning democracy avoids [the excessive capital accumulation] not by the redistribution of income to those with less at the end of each period, so to speak, but rather by ensuring the widespread ownership of productive assets and human capital

[52] Freeman (2007, 223–224).
[53] See also Gilens (2005).
[54] Freeman (2007).
[55] Schefczyk (2013).
[56] Hacker (2011, 35).
[57] O'Neill (2020).

[...] at the beginning of each period".[58] Rawls acknowledges the crucial distinction between the tools of the welfare state in market economies and the background institutions in POD: "one major difference is this: the background institutions of property-owning democracy work to disperse the ownership of wealth and capital, and thus to prevent a small part of society from controlling the economy, and indirectly, political life as well. By contrast, welfare state capitalism permits a small class to have a near monopoly of the means of production".[59]

There is no questioning of the existence of property rights, but rather a recognition of the need to regulate the relationship between property rights and the processes of accumulation in a market economy. And there is recognition of the welfare state's inability to limit the concentration of wealth in the hands of a few, because its aim "is that none should fall below a decent minimum standard of life [...]. The redistribution of income serves this purpose when, at the end of each period, those who need assistance can be identified".[60] The task of modifying income and wealth distributions cannot be left solely to the traditional redistributive tools of a tax-and-transfer state. Tax-and-transfer systems, as compensatory mechanisms designed to address inequality, are only a partial and flawed solution, one that preserves market democracy. To some extent, these systems serve as a safe haven for neoliberalism, offering redistribution without altering the underlying causes of inequality. Moreover, they expose individuals to the risk of sudden shifts in both taxes and transfers—more so than would be the case for public goods and services.

In a different perspective, predistribution presents itself as a potent concept, as it should encompass the full range of state laws, regulations, and policies, with particular emphasis on corporate governance law, trade union law, patent law, regulation of public utilities, and, not least, the regulation of the largely unregulated financial sector. The absence of such regulation is precisely what has allowed neoliberalism to quietly construct a "conservative nanny state", with income concentration as one of its manifestations.[61] In the following sections, we will elaborate on the basic institutions of the social contract required by a DWS, which together form

[58] Rawls (2001, 139).
[59] Rawls (2001, 139).
[60] Rawls (2001, 140).
[61] Baker (2006).

a framework of predistribution capable of reasserting a substantial role for the political constitution. The policies outlined below form a framework that goes beyond mere taxation and transfer mechanisms, aiming instead to shape the primary distribution of income and power within the economic system. They represent an effort to reconcile the concept of predistribution with the pursuit of "broadly progressive or egalitarian goals".[62]

The Tax System in a Democratic Welfare State

In a POD, the structure of taxation is designed to reflect the fundamental necessity of ensuring equal opportunities, thus preventing the emergence of large inequalities. Consequently, the need for extraordinary tax measures aimed at compensating for such undesirable outcomes would not arise. In a POD there would be no significant disparities in income and wealth among individuals; however, if such disparities do occur, Rawls posits that the most appropriate tool for addressing them would be an inheritance (and gift) tax, designed to limit the intergenerational transmission of wealth and income.[63]

However, the inheritance tax cannot be regarded as a stable or primary source of tax revenue. Rather, its objective is to disperse wealth and income. As a result, Rawls contends that there would no longer be any significant issue if capital owners wished to distribute their estate prior to their death. In other words, within Rawls's framework, an inheritance tax is necessary as part of an ordinary tax system but should not be considered a recurrent revenue source, as its effect is to fragment the concentration of wealth before it is taxed. This is a subtle distinction, but one that is crucial for policy purposes; namely, that inheritance tax should not be relied upon to permanently finance public spending. As it stands, WSC proves to be an unsatisfactory model because, in most cases, the inheritance tax is applied with significant exemptions and exclusions, thus failing in both its function of revenue collection and its role in limiting the concentration of wealth and income in line with Rawlsian principles.

In POD, the limited concentration of income and wealth does not necessitate a progressive structure for income taxation. As outlined by Rawls, both inheritance taxes and progressive income taxes (when deemed

[62] O'Neill (2020, 74). See also Hacker (2011).
[63] Rawls (1999, 245–251); Rawls (2001, 160–161).

necessary) are crucial for upholding the institutions of equal liberty in a POD (the first principle) and ensuring the fair value of the rights they establish.[64] While this position has often been viewed as critical and surprising within the Rawlsian model, it is, in fact, not.[65] The progressivity of the income tax is required only in cases of 'unjust distributions'—distributions of income and wealth in which neither income nor wealth is sufficiently dispersed. Therefore, a progressive income tax may serve as a temporary measure, implemented until the concentration of income and wealth has been sufficiently reduced. As clearly stated, the aim of such levies "is not to raise revenue [...] but gradually and continually to correct the distribution of wealth and to prevent concentrations of power detrimental to the fair value of political liberty and fair equality of opportunity".[66] Since a set of public institutions is required to ensure equal opportunities for education and culture for all citizens, and to keep positions and offices accessible to everyone based on merit and effort, the primary objective of taxes is to prevent these institutions from being jeopardized when wealth inequalities exceed a certain threshold. Thus, it is not surprising that, once the basic institutions are in place to guarantee equal opportunities, the tax system that Rawls envisions in a fully operational POD is an expenditure tax of Kaldorian nature,[67] which might even be proportional, as this type of tax is fundamentally designed to ensure the financing of public goods and to safeguard the fair equality of opportunities (the second principle). The main justification for such a tax is that individuals would be taxed based on what they withdraw from the economic system (consumption), rather than on what they contribute to (incomes).

It is also important to note that, in Rawls's framework, the size of the public sector is not inherently problematic. Citizens may choose to allocate further public expenditures beyond those necessary to ensure equality of opportunity. Rawls does not overlook the possibility that the size of the public sector might exceed what is necessary to ensure equality of opportunity. In this case, the additional expenditure would be financed through the application of the benefit principle.[68] In this regard, the size of the public sector would depend on the relative valuations that citizens place

64 Rawls (1999, 247).
65 Fried (2003).
66 Rawls (1999, 245).
67 Kaldor (1955). For a discussion of consumption taxation in Rawls, see Elkins (2019).
68 Rawls (1999, 250–251).

on public versus private goods. This concept is crucial for our argument, as it provides a theoretical justification for linking taxes to public spending. It makes plausible the idea that, in the ordinary functioning of a tax system, both the ability-to-pay principle and the benefit principle can coexist.

Regardless of whether an expenditure tax and an income tax can serve as alternative instruments, one essential feature they must share is that they must be general, meaning that no one should have the option to opt out of the tax system. This would represent a direct application of Rawls's assertion that "[w]e are not to gain from the cooperative efforts of others without doing our fair share".[69] Here, "our fair share" implies that if everyone benefits from the social contract, which guarantees basic liberties and equal opportunities, then each individual must contribute their "fair share" of taxes. It follows that, whatever the form of taxation (whether an expenditure or income tax), any loophole that is not directly related to the proper measurement of ability to pay must be avoided. Furthermore, the access to public services should be universally available, provided that individuals have paid their fair share of taxes. This would exclude means-testing in the provision of benefits and would address a key criticism of WSC in the Rawlsian framework: that society is divided according to income sources (private vs. public sector). Consequently, our concept of DWS should be based on a comprehensive income tax, the closure of any exit options from the tax system, and the provision of universal free access to welfare state provisions. The alignment between taxes paid and universal welfare state benefits would be an initial step towards approximating POD and curbing the concentration of wealth and income due to preferential tax treatments.

At this point, a clarification is needed regarding how we understand tax policy within the context of DWS. On the one hand, our tax system does not fully conform to the equitable taxation (ET) theory, because, in its basic functioning, it separates taxes from public spending.[70] In the ET framework, taxation is based solely on the ability-to-pay principle, without considering the benefit principle. Since benefit taxation is not applicable, a different method of taxation had to be devised to raise revenue. Simons,

[69] Rawls (1999, 301).

[70] Simons (1938). Equitable taxation is a principle of fiscal justice grounded in the idea that taxation should apply fairly to individuals' ability to pay, measured in terms of comprehensive income—that is, the sum of consumption and the net change in wealth over a given period.

who introduced the concept of comprehensive taxation, alongside Haig and Schanz, disregarded in the ET theory the benefits provided by public spending.[71] Instead, this is central to our conception of DWS. Despite this difference, both DWS and ET share the need for a general tax on all income sources. However, since the ability to pay, according to some scholars of the ET tradition, may be most accurately represented by consumption, it can be argued that ET theory, to some extent, approximates Rawls's concept of an expenditure tax. This is especially relevant because ET focuses primarily on horizontal equity, while issues of vertical equity are left to the political process. Such an outcome can, at least partially, justify the adoption of a proportional (flat) tax.

In the framework of the DWS, a significant distinction can be made with respect to the optimal taxation scheme. As previously discussed, this scheme is firmly rooted in public economics and framed within a general equilibrium setting in a second-best environment. Its structure is characterized by a constrained optimization problem aimed at maximizing a social welfare function. In this context, optimal taxation emphasizes the relevance of the deadweight loss of taxation, and governments are typically assumed to be exogenous. As such, optimal taxation does not emerge from a social contract but rather assumes that collective choice can be mediated through the social welfare function. By prioritizing efficiency, the size of the public sector is implicitly determined, a feature that closely mirrors the functioning of market democracy. Consequently, any social contract that deviates from what is permitted by these technical conditions is, in effect, null and void.

Similarly, a comparable distinction can be made with respect to the Fiscal Exchange (FE) theory of taxation.[72] The central issue in the origins of FE was the design of governmental institutions that could align with the electorate (presumed to be driven by the social contract) while ensuring that the electoral process would not lead to exploitation by interest groups. These concerns, to some extent, align with the general structure of POD; however, over time, FE has shifted its focus towards limiting the power of potentially malevolent governments, in the context of public choice theory.[73] In this view, the state is seen as a Leviathan seeking to maximize

[71] Haig (1921); Schanz (1896).

[72] For a more comprehensive treatment of ET, OT, and FE, see Hettich and Winer (1999).

[73] Buchanan (1976); Brennan and Buchanan (1980).

the extraction of resources from its citizens. Consequently, constitutional rules are deemed necessary to constrain the Leviathan-like tendencies of governments. This perspective tends to praise constitutional rules for ensuring that the level and types of public services provided match the preferences of the electorate. However, there is no justification for a social contract that is based on the presumed malice of one of the contracting parties, yet still ensures maximum benefits for all.

The DWS framework fundamentally departs from this assumption. We contend that the tax system should be the result of a fiscal contract made on equal terms, rather than a by-product of a social contract constrained by the opportunistic behaviour of one of the parties. The presence of opportunism, in fact, undermines the very foundation of the social contract, which would render all the defining characteristics of DWS null and void. Indeed, when political authority is weak, powerful groups tend to pressure governments to refrain from imposing high taxes, even when these are intended to fund social solidarity programs. The primary goal of DWS is precisely to prevent opportunism and special interests from dominating the social contract. A democratic conception of society is one in which a system of cooperation among equals prevails,[74] and this is also the underlying basis of the tax system in the DWS framework.

Education, Health, Housing, and the Labour Market in a Democratic Welfare State

General Framework

On the expenditure side, certain provisions of the traditional welfare state still play a crucial role in ensuring equality of opportunity, limiting the concentration of power, and addressing inequality at its roots. In this regard, the DWS places particular emphasis on healthcare, education, and housing. These areas can be seen as components of a broader strategy of social investment aimed at enhancing access to the labour market and at promoting social cohesion. They also represent a predistributive alternative to conventional tax-and-transfer mechanisms, with the ultimate goal of reducing income inequality.

Nevertheless, it must be acknowledged that the provision of healthcare, education, and housing services necessarily requires tax resources. The key

[74] Rawls (1999), especially chapter 1.

distinction, however, lies in the economic rationale behind such funding: taxes that support predistributive tools are tied to the provision of specific public services based on a rights-based approach, rather than to monetary transfers directed at the most disadvantaged groups under a needs-based approach. General taxation is necessary not merely to redistribute income, but to ensure universal access to essential services. The public provision of these services—alongside transportation and public utilities—constitutes the foundational conditions within which various social groups negotiate their economic relationships and positions in society.[75]

Progressive taxation can play a dual role: not only can it finance predistributive public spending, but it may also function as a predistributive mechanism in its own right, fostering the conditions for genuine equality of opportunity. As previously noted, tax progressivity can be understood as a form of differential pricing for universal public services (see chapter 2). The combined effect of a general progressive tax system and the inherently equalizing impact of universal service provision may contribute to reshaping *ex ante* market income distribution, thereby reducing the need for *ex post* redistribution. Conversely, if wealthier citizens opt out of public provision in favour of private alternatives—a do-it-yourself dynamic—this may undermine both universal programmes and the tax base required to sustain them. Such a shift risks leading to a residual model of the welfare state, characterized by weakened universalism and diminished redistributive capacity.

In what follows we provide the main arguments why education, health, housing programmes, and a regulation of the labour market are essential for the development of DWS. Although there may appear to be little novelty compared to traditional welfare state interventions, a profound distinction lies in how these interventions are conceptualized—and, consequently, in the imperative to prioritize them based on rights rather than needs. For this shift to be fully realized, access to services must be universal—no longer contingent on means-testing—and also for this reason they must not be hindered by the diversion of tax revenues toward preferential fiscal treatments for specific segments of the population, which undermines principles of reciprocity and mutuality.[76]

[75] O'Neill (2020, 77).

[76] For a treatment of welfare rights in the context of the United Nations Declaration of Human Rights, see Watson (2009). See the discussion in Offe (1987, 527), who also argues

Education

With specific regard to education, the main objective of DWS is to implement comprehensive models that promote social mobility, serving as a preventive measure to the development of high social inequalities. Investments in education have traditionally been uncontroversial in social democratic systems, despite the fact that various governments have, over time, pursued alternative paths.[77] What can be gleaned from existing literature is that investments in human capital may yield economic growth effects even more substantial than those resulting from investments in physical capital.[78] Generally speaking, the argument suggests that more skilled individuals contribute to the rapid adoption of new technologies and production processes, a characteristic of endogenous growth models.[79] Consequently, disparities in cognitive skills can lead to significant differences in economic growth. If this is the case, the obvious policy implication is that educational policies must be effective in enhancing cognitive skills—an issue often underestimated in its capacity to mitigate the demand shift away from unskilled workers and the weakening of the low-skilled labour market, which has contributed to increased pay dispersion and worklessness in recent decades.[80]

Policies aimed at raising skills would indeed have a dual positive effect on inequality: on one hand, they would enhance the quality of labour in the lower segments of the income distribution; on the other hand, they would increase the supply of educated labour at the top of the income distribution, thus lowering the education wage premium.[81] Both effects would contribute to a reduction in inequality, while also narrowing the achievement gap between children from low-income families and those from more affluent backgrounds. This phenomenon, first observed in the UK, has also been noted in other countries and plays a significant role in the persistence of inequality and in differences in long-term equality of

that "[t]he disorganization of broad, relatively stable, and encompassing commonalities of economic interest, associational affiliation, or cultural values and life-styles is [...] the key to an adequate understanding of the general weakening of solidaristic commitments".

[77] Huber and Stephens (2015, 67).

[78] Hanushek and Woessmann (2012).

[79] Romer (1990).

[80] Nickell (2004, C24).

[81] Huber and Stephens (2015, 68).

opportunity.[82] As also emphasized, human capital acquired through access to education is a critical form of property.[83] Indeed, large disparities in human capital may set the stage for long-term inequalities in assets or income.

This underscores the importance of predistributive educational policies aimed at closing these gaps through social investments. Even conservative estimates of the returns on early childhood education suggest that they are among the most productive investments governments can make, not least because of the strong link between education and productivity in adulthood.[84] Moreover, this perspective explains why other scholars have contended that public policies should not focus solely on narrow goals of academic excellence, but rather on maximizing the capacity of every individual to lead an independent life and transition smoothly from education to the labour market.[85] This is a crucial element in ensuring the stability of the social contract. Accordingly, within a DWS framework, investments in education must prioritize early childhood education as a core area of social investment—not least because a structural shift is necessary in contrast to the traditional welfare state, which has succeeded in addressing old-age poverty but has invested too little (and too late) in the younger generations.[86]

If there is something to be learned from the most advanced welfare state models—particularly the Nordic model—it is that education has been not only treated as a key policy instrument to support children from low-income families in accessing higher levels of education, but also complemented by vocational education and training (VET) programmes integrated into comprehensive secondary education.[87] VET, in fact, is regarded as an important tool for improving the relative income position of low-skilled workers, thereby helping to close the earnings gap between more and less educated individuals. In this regard, it is important to note the strong link between educational attainment and employment rates. According to OECD data (2022), the average employment rate

[82] West (2007).
[83] Williamson (2013).
[84] Heckman et al. (2013); Hacker (2015).
[85] Fishkin (2014).
[86] Tsarouhas (2015); Wade (2013).
[87] Busemeyer (2015).

in OECD countries rises with educational attainment: among individuals aged 25–64, the employment rate is 59% for those without upper secondary education, 77% for those with upper secondary or post-secondary non-tertiary education, and 86% for those with tertiary education. Moreover, high-quality vocational education can facilitate the transition from school to work: among young adults aged 25–34, the employment rate is 83% for those with vocational qualifications at the upper secondary or post-secondary level, compared to 73% for those with a general education at the same level.

To ensure positive outcomes in terms of predistributive inequality, an essential requirement is the availability of sufficient tax revenues to finance an extensive and inclusive educational system. On this basis, the DWS relies on the predominance of public funding as a necessary precondition for education to realize its full potential. As previously discussed, the DWS framework depends on general taxation to minimize reliance on *ex post* redistribution. Historical evidence from traditional welfare states shows that the share of private funding in education has been consistently low in Scandinavian countries and relatively high in liberal Anglo-Saxon systems. It has been observed a positive correlation between social inequality—measured by the Gini index—and the private share of tertiary education funding during the period 1998–2008. Several factors may explain this outcome, but one is particularly relevant here: higher tuition fees may discourage students from lower-income backgrounds from pursuing higher education, thus reinforcing educational and social inequalities. The expansion of private financing in education may have indirect and problematic consequences. In particular, public support for government intervention in education tends to be lower in countries with high levels of private spending.[88] Individuals who have financed their own education are typically less willing to pay taxes to support others, perceiving taxation as a threat to the returns on their educational investment and to their privileged, monopolistic access. This attitude contributes to maintaining barriers to education and hinders social mobility, thereby preserving existing class structures.

Given the widespread presence of private funding across OECD countries, reversing this trend will require time—another reason why social investment must begin at the earliest stages of the educational pathway.

[88] Busemeyer (2015).

Since the design of educational institutions plays a crucial role in mitigating inequality, public policy can shape societal attitudes and challenges the perception that inequality is merely the inevitable outcome of impersonal market forces. After all, this is not a new concept. As has already been argued in the past, "[t]here is no extravagance more prejudicial to the growth of national wealth than that wasteful negligence which allows genius that happens to be born of lowly parentage to expend itself in lowly work. No change would conduce so much to a rapid increase of material wealth as an improvement in our schools [...] provided it be combined with an extensive system of scholarships, which will enable the clever son of a working man to rise gradually from school to school till he has the best theoretical and practical education which the age can give".[89] Accordingly, the core principle of the DWS is to allocate equal public resources to the education of all children as a matter of rights.[90] To this end, disparities in funding across territories should be avoided, as they risk fostering educational segregation—often rooted in patterns of residential segregation—which, as will be discussed below, underscores the need for a coherent and supportive housing policy.

Health

To reverse the priorities of market democracy, substantial public funding for healthcare is required in order to ensure equality of opportunity, regardless of health-related events over the course of the life cycle. In this case as well, tax revenues are necessary to finance universal healthcare provisions; once again, the correspondence between taxation and public spending is essential to sustain a viable social contract. This general principle is especially compelling for individuals suffering from chronic illness or disabilities, who are not in a position to fully realize their potential compared to equally talented individuals without such conditions.[91] To this observation, one can add that even individuals with equal abilities may be unable to perform at the same level if they live in disadvantaged socio-economic contexts. It follows that when health systems are dominated

[89] Marshall (1920/1947, 212). An earlier statement on the need to go beyond a system of scholarships and move toward making all levels of education free of charge, see also Rossi (1946), especially chapter 6.

[90] Williamson (2013).

[91] Freeman (2007).

by private provision, resources are allocated through market mechanisms, which may lead to the rationing of healthcare based on the ability to pay. In such cases, no genuine social contract is in place, and it is likely that wealthier individuals will receive better care than poorer ones—just as they are more likely to receive better education.

By contrast, in systems where the public sector is involved in healthcare provision, it is often suggested that some form of rationing reflects what citizens are collectively willing to fund through taxation. However, this framing of the issue reduces healthcare provision to a matter of individual preferences. In contrast, the DWS perspective is grounded in rights rather than preferences: healthcare should be universally guaranteed, regardless of individuals' preferences. In any case, no form of rationing should apply until all basic healthcare needs and treatments are guaranteed to everyone. In this regard, although access to healthcare for all in need is widely considered a fundamental social right—and is central to the assessment of health systems—the European context, despite its long-standing tradition of social protection, only appears to guarantee universal coverage. As shown in a recent empirical study covering most European countries,[92] there remain significant inequalities in healthcare access both within and across countries. Even where (near -) universal access has been formally achieved, this does not necessarily translate into equitable usage. Access may vary significantly depending on geographic location (spatial opportunity), the timing of health needs, economic affordability (especially where public systems do not ensure full coverage), and individual characteristics. These barriers—commonly referred to as unmet needs—seriously undermine the effectiveness and fairness of healthcare systems.

In particular, when examining unmet healthcare needs more directly linked to budget constraints, long waiting lists, and travel costs to reach medical facilities, it becomes evident that these are disproportionately concentrated among lower-income individuals across most European systems. Moreover, income-related unmet needs arising from financial barriers are primarily driven by economic factors—such as the share of out-of-pocket health expenditure—whereas those linked to long waiting times and travel-related costs are more closely associated with institutional factors.

As a matter of fact, many European countries fail to guarantee equal access to treatments or prescribed medications irrespective of income level.

[92] Carnazza et al. (2023).

Even in countries with health systems based on universal access, individuals with lower incomes often do not receive equal care. This suggests that the principle of universalism has increasingly been eroded in favour of market-based logic—a shift that the DWS model seeks to counteract. What is currently occurring in the healthcare systems of the most developed parts of the world is a process of downsizing that cannot be justified by the traditional cost-effectiveness rationale, as many healthcare services that are demonstrably cost-effective are no longer provided by the public sector. Hence, the core issue is not how to define the threshold for cost-effectiveness, but rather why cost-effective measures are not being made universally accessible. It is precisely this concern that lies at the heart of the DWS approach.

In this context, it must be acknowledged that traditional healthcare models have long relied on the outsourcing of services to private companies and third-sector organizations. However, the recent evolution of the purchaser—provider split—where public entities fund services while private actors deliver them—has significantly increased the risk that collective security (i.e., the availability of services free of charge at the point of use) may be undermined. As a result, increasing levels of privatization and the growing availability of private alternatives may threaten the social contract embedded in the traditional welfare state. These concerns are further reinforced by the observation that the public sector—much like in other domains of market democracy—is often ill-equipped to negotiate effectively with private companies. This contributes to the perception that welfare states have become "easy pickings for boosting corporate profits", thereby "weakening public accountability and institutional responsibility".[93]

Housing

In DWS, housing ownership can play a pivotal role in equipping individuals with a share of capital assets, thereby fostering dignity, autonomy, and self-respect.[94] To some extent, this form of asset ownership is easier to provide than shares in entrepreneurial ventures, and it directly addresses a fundamental need that often remains unmet due to insufficient private

[93] Gamble (2015, 29).
[94] Williamson (2013).

resources. The expansion of public housing would also help alleviate pressure on the rental market, thereby lowering rental prices in the private sector. As documented in the British context—a pattern observable in other European countries as well—private landlords have frequently denied individuals the right to decent housing by capitalizing on the scarcity of building land and rental properties.[95]

A key challenge in this domain lies in the choice between two approaches: either ensuring that everyone pays a fair market price—with fairness achieved via rent and rate rebates—or directly providing publicly funded social housing. This dilemma is far from new. Housing has historically been referred to as the "wobbly pillar of the welfare state",[96] due to the persistent tendency to delegate its provision to the private sector. Yet, some scholars have argued that decommodification can only be realized through direct state provision of housing.[97] Furthermore, decent housing is a fundamental determinant of health, even though national healthcare systems—especially in Europe—have often overlooked the housing dimension in their planning and delivery.

Despite housing being clearly within the domain of life-sustaining goods, the responsibility for its provision remains legally ambiguous, as it is unclear who is accountable for guaranteeing a legally enforceable right to housing.[98] Additionally, public provision often falls short of what is commonly considered a reasonable standard.[99] As previously discussed in relation to education, housing segregation should be avoided, as it tends to reinforce both income and educational segregation. This reinforces the argument that housing policy cannot be designed or implemented in isolation from other components of a DWS. Historical evidence supports this view. For instance, studies have shown a close link between homelessness and welfare regimes:[100] in particular, regimes that "produce high levels of poverty and inequality not only produce high levels of homelessness, but the resulting homeless population is made up predominantly of households facing access and affordability problems".[101] In the US, for example, the

[95] Lowe and Jones (2002).
[96] Torgersen (1987).
[97] Harloe (1995); Groves et al. (2007).
[98] Marshall (1965).
[99] Torgersen (1987, 118).
[100] Fitzpatrick (1998).
[101] Stephens and Fitzpatrick (2007, 209).

rise in homelessness during the 1980s has been attributed largely to the decline in housing affordability for households at the lower end of the income distribution.[102]

These findings suggest that WSC alone may not suffice to guarantee housing as a right, and that reliance on private provision for all households may lead to systematic market failure. In such cases, the public sector is often called upon to correct these failures *ex post*. However, from a DWS perspective, planned *ex ante* public housing policies would better serve to remove one of the most significant barriers to achieving equality of opportunity.

The Labour Market

In a market democracy, a flexible labour market is a primary source of inequality. Such flexibility becomes more feasible as political representation and the strength of trade unions become increasingly fragmented. Over the past decades, this fragmentation has contributed to a decoupling of median wage growth from productivity increases. As a result, the benefits of enhanced production efficiency have not been equitably shared between workers and capital owners.[103] In particular, a sustained race to the bottom in real unit labour costs has been observed across many OECD countries over the past four decades.[104] Globalization has further contributed to this dynamic by enabling a flexible reallocation of capital in search of higher returns. This has weakened centralized collective bargaining systems and led to a decline in union density.[105] In Europe, this trend has been exacerbated by the enlargement of the European Union to include Eastern European countries—regions typically characterized by low unionization rates and lower labour costs. These factors have made them attractive locations for relocating production from Western European countries with higher wages and more extensive welfare systems.

Trade unions play a crucial role in balancing the bargaining power between employers and workers. Within the framework of the DWS, an equitable distribution of bargaining power is fundamental to addressing

[102] Quigley and Raphael (2001).
[103] Flecker (2010).
[104] Kiefer and Rada (2015).
[105] Swank (2002).

inequality at its roots. Trade unions also help to limit the concentration of political power, especially when they succeed in fostering robust links among political parties, unions, and civil society—a set of connections that has markedly weakened across the industrialized world in recent decades.[106] In the same vein, rebalancing the bargaining power between labour and capital is also essential to curbing the influence of corporate interests through large-scale lobbying efforts. It is arguably no coincidence that the decline in union density observed in many countries has been accompanied by the erosion of a middle class historically aligned with lower-income groups and traditionally supportive of welfare state policies. Furthermore, workers' participation in the production process has significantly diminished, as evidenced by the steady decline in union density since 1980.

Market democracy has fostered the return to the commodification of labour, in stark contrast to the decommodification that was foundational to the development of welfare states.[107] Commodification plays a key role in shaping inequality: for instance, young people who experience prolonged unemployment or frequent periods out of work tend to face higher future unemployment risks and lower wages when employed,[108] thereby contributing to a cumulative effect that exacerbates inequality. Commodification also runs counter to the Rawlsian principle of equal basic liberties, as it makes an individual's access to economic resources contingent on the discretion of employers—a dependency that a system of cooperative democracy should aim to eliminate. A crucial issue in this regard is the definition of a social minimum. Within market democracies, WSC tends to rely on minimum wage mechanisms, focusing primarily on efficiency outcomes rather than the needs of the least advantaged. In Rawls's POD, social assistance *per se* does not take precedence. Rawls argues that a just society should not necessarily provide a social minimum to individuals who, for example, choose to surf rather than work. In line with the emphasis on individual responsibility embedded in POD, Rawls proposes that individuals who voluntarily opt out of employment "should have the monetary value of a normal work subtracted from the social minimum that the least advantaged normally receive [...] So in a sense,

[106] Tsarouhas (2015, 149).
[107] Esping-Andersen (1990).
[108] Gregg (2015).

the surfer is provided with what many may call 'welfare', but the monetary sum he receives is less than he would receive if he chose to work."[109]

This position aligns with support for active labour market policies over passive monetary transfers. Rawls also maintains that individuals may contribute to social cooperation in ways other than through formal employment. Able-bodied individuals who choose not to work are not acting unjustly, provided they fulfil other civic obligations—such as obeying the law, performing public duties, or engaging in voluntary or charitable work. From this perspective, the social minimum is not simply "money for doing nothing"; rather, it reflects a broader notion of reciprocal contribution. A non-working citizen's lifestyle may be worthy of the same respect as that of an "equally unproductive leisurely well-to-do" who pays his fair share of taxes.[110] Under this view, the surfer could still be entitled to a monetary transfer.

In real-world economies, determining the appropriate structure for a social minimum, basic income, or minimum wage is complex. Nevertheless, it is possible to define the conditions under which such a minimum could be realized within a DWS framework. A DWS model would include a monetary threshold below which no one would fall—regardless of their employment status. Crucially, the social minimum must be grounded in the idea of reciprocity, enabling citizens to view themselves as free and equal, and to regard society as a fair system of cooperation over time. In this sense, the social minimum should be reflected in the tax system as a non-taxable base income available to all taxpayers—whether through income tax exemptions or targeted expenditure measures. This approach could also serve to set a benchmark for the minimum wage, thereby reinforcing the decommodification of labour.

Fiscal Democracy in a Fragmented Society

Behind the celebrated narrative of globalization as a triumph of liberal democracy, the classical nineteenth-century dichotomy between the freedom of the ancients and the freedom of the moderns—that is, between freedom from the state and freedom in the state—appears to have been ultimately resolved. In this outcome, the concept of freedom from the state

[109] Freeman (2007, 229–230).
[110] Freeman (2007, 230).

emerges as the dominant one, infused with a renewed spirit akin to that championed by Constant in opposition to Rousseau: a freedom defined by the individual's right to peacefully enjoy independence of movement, communication, and economic exchange, all within a political order subordinated to a globalized economic order driven by the market's capacity to generate and diffuse prosperity. Nor does belief in this capacity of the market appear to have been seriously challenged by the recent protectionist and nationalist reactions to globalization, which, paradoxically, celebrates the prominence of the very same economic-technological elites. In market democracy, universal suffrage becomes democracy's sole meaningful content, while equality is reframed as an impediment to the flourishing of merit, innovation, and individual capabilities—qualities the market is presumed uniquely capable of identifying and rewarding, bounded only by the principle of free competition. To achieve competitive efficiency for the benefit of society, the market demands the fragmentation of economic agents. Consequently, the democratic processes of aggregating and representing collective preferences through intermediate bodies are portrayed as incompatible with the unimpeded operation of markets. In fact, the fragmentation of collective preferences is a defining feature of market democracy. Formal democracy—embodied in universal suffrage—exhausts the substance of democracy, relegating questions of substantive equality to the market. The weaker and more fragmented the intermediate institutions, the more universal suffrage reinforces the fragmentation of preferences.[111] The crisis of traditional political parties has largely unfolded in parallel with the trajectory of globalization, whereby the diffusion of an economic model based on the fragmentation of production processes has mirrored the disintegration of political representation.

Political fragmentation entails a loss of representational power for citizens and a corresponding empowerment of market forces, which increasingly shape, and even dominate, political decision-making. Along this trajectory, democracy risks falling not merely under the influence, but under the control of those who wield market power. When public preferences are fragmented, politics ceases to make a tangible difference in the lives of citizens. This can foster a widespread perception of "deadlock, incompetence, and corruption among what seems an increasingly self-contained and self-serving political class", thereby reinforcing the belief

[111] Hirschman (1990).

that "there is no alternative" to the market—wherein market processes are viewed as superior to political processes—and contributing to declining electoral participation.[112]

Available data on voter turnout worldwide suggest that abstention rates are disproportionately composed of low-income voters and segments of the middle class. Consequently, low voter turnout may serve as an indicator of social domination and procedural unfairness in electoral systems. It can result in unrepresentative governments, policy decisions that fail to reflect the preferences of the majority, and a general erosion of the legitimacy of elected officials. According to 2022 data from the *International Institute for Democracy and Electoral Assistance*, among OECD countries, voter turnout exceeded 70% only in Belgium, South Korea, Australia, and the Netherlands. Germany, France, Italy, and Spain recorded rates between 65 and 69%, while the USs and the UK remained at 62%, and both Japan and Canada fell below 60%. In the US, based on various indicators—such as voter registration, representation and participation, voting access, election security, and institutional integrity—only four states achieved a high overall policy rating; 11 were rated low, while 35 states received either medium or fair ratings.

Whether political systems can become more responsive to declining turnout remains a matter of debate.[113] Nonetheless, low electoral participation may reasonably be interpreted as a symptom of political and social fragmentation within a market democracy. When collective preferences are fragmented, they lack the capacity to bring about significant change to the socio-economic and political *status quo*, which is often upheld by narratives invoking impersonal market forces or by supranational entities with limited democratic accountability. To some extent, the market operates independently of democratic institutions—and is, in fact, fundamentally indifferent, if not hostile, to them.[114] Market economy and democracy appeared compatible only during the Cold War, when the existence of a viable alternative to capitalism necessitated some degree of alignment.[115] Times have now changed profoundly, and a widespread narrative has taken shape around the alleged incompatibility between freedom and

[112] Streeck (2016, 40).
[113] Ezrow and Krause (2023).
[114] Fitoussi (2004, 11).
[115] Streeck (2016).

democracy, and between the market and democratic governance. This narrative has prompted calls for a retreat from politics—more specifically, from the obligations of the social contract and from the political, social, and economic institutions that allocate rights and duties within a community and determine the fair distribution of the benefits of social cooperation. In the view advanced by segments of the financial oligarchy, freedom is equated not with civic participation but with market autonomy. From this perspective, democracy imposes constraints on competition and redistribution, while the market is believed to distribute outcomes efficiently—and thus justly—without the need for political mediation. To this end, democracy is increasingly expected to resolve itself into the market—guaranteeing individuals the freedom to enter and exit economic arrangements for their own benefit. In this model, the citizen's democratic agency is reinterpreted as the ability to "vote with one's feet" in the marketplace. Yet, since the possibility of exit without cost is constrained by the coercive nature of citizenship and the high price of opting out (ranging from migration to, in extreme cases, revolt), the fragmentation of collective preferences and intermediate political bodies has extended to the state itself. This fragmentation of states has occurred through the proliferation of free economic and fiscal zones—such as tax havens, free ports, duty-free districts, and special economic zones, in which "the zone was not merely the means to an economic end, but an inspiration for a reorganization of global politics as a whole";[116]

The free zones operate as enclaves that are wholly or partially exempt from regulatory obligations and fiscal duties, instead offering preferential treatment to investors or transnational corporations—many of which can thereby conceal or significantly reduce taxation on profits. The size of such enclaves varies, sometimes extending over the entire territory of a state or city-state. The number of such zones has reached approximately 5,400 and continues to grow, driven by competition among jurisdictions that increasingly view these enclaves as key contributors to national prosperity.[117] Along this path of silent secession from political authority, the dissolution of the social contract and the rise of the market as the *de facto*

[116] Slobodian (2023, 7). As also stated by Thiel (2009), "because there are no truly free places left in our world, I suspect that the mode for escape must involve some sort of new and hitherto untried process that leads us to some undiscovered country".

[117] Slobodian (2023, 3).

solution to political failure have quietly advanced. This transformation involves the systematic erosion of reciprocity in the distribution of the benefits and burdens of cooperation among free and equal individuals. It raises profound questions about the stability of both reciprocity and cooperation in international relations—namely, whether societies respect the foundational political, social, and economic institutions of others, which are essential to sustaining mutually beneficial and reciprocal collaboration. Those who relocate productive activities to free zones in host countries and benefit from preferential tax regimes are often in a privileged position: they enjoy the basic institutional framework guaranteed by local systems of cooperation and reciprocity while contributing less than residents. In this way, the benefits of cooperation are asymmetrically shared, violating the principle of reciprocity.[118] The case of digital companies is even more extreme: they appropriate various forms of collective resources and rely on a wide range of publicly funded infrastructures—such as internet networks, energy systems, legal frameworks, and public education that provides skilled labour—without contributing proportionally, through taxation, to the benefits they receive. In this context, they operate within a kind of global free zone, where the fiscal contract is not merely suspended but entirely non-existent. Nonetheless, it remains possible to re-establish this contract through tax schemes that reflect the relationship between benefits received and the ability to pay, given the clear evidence of the advantages digital companies derive from the communities in which they operate.

While it is often argued that the economic contributions made by those who exploit free zones outweigh the fiscal advantages they receive, this logic inherently institutes a regime of exception. It leads to the dissolution of the fiscal contract and the fragmentation of the social contract in a multiplicity of arrangements, in which certain actors contribute only partially to the costs of social cooperation while maintaining full access to its benefits. As a result, this fragmentation undermines the foundational trust that all members of society are equally committed to a fair system of mutual cooperation. Ultimately, the stability of the social contract is fundamentally

[118] Once the existence of the benefits that these firms derive from operating within a given state is acknowledged, Freeman's argument holds that these firms should be considered members of that national society and therefore ought to contribute "their fair share toward socially productive cooperation according to the rules of the basic social institutions that regulate the political and economic relations of, and claim jurisdiction over and allegiance from, all members of the same society". See Freeman (2018, 214).

compromised. As we discussed, tax havens are equally disruptive to the stability of the social contract. At the international level, all forms of tax havens undermine the basic institutions of other countries. This occurs, for example, when transnational corporations shift corporate profits abroad, thereby removing tax revenues essential for financing fundamental social rights in their countries of origin—such as housing, healthcare, and education described above. The issue becomes even more paradoxical when tax havens operate within common markets or supranational unions, as is the case with the Netherlands, Luxembourg, and Cyprus within the European Union. In such instances, the funding of essential public institutions in these countries is achieved, at least in part (if not entirely), by depriving other member states of the same union of the fiscal resources necessary to sustain their own public services. This process replicates, at the international level, a pattern already observable within national borders: universal public services are financed by some but enjoyed by others who benefit from fiscal privileges—constituting a clear violation of the principle of reciprocity.

Accordingly, transnational corporations move not where their productivity is most valued, but where preferential tax treatment yields the highest return—essentially engaging in a form of free riding. The fragmentation of fiscal rules mirrors a deeper fragmentation of the foundational institutions and social rights a community seeks to guarantee. Without clearly defining the perimeter of social rights—either nationally or internationally—the tax system becomes a lawless terrain, where actors are incentivized to exit its jurisdiction by establishing new ones and severing their obligations to the broader community. For this reason, international agreements cannot begin by defining a common tax unless there is first a clearly defined common framework of social rights. It should therefore be evident that recent initiatives, such as the Global Minimum Tax (GMT) or the G20's proposal to tax the super-rich, may be considered weak agreements. They approach the issue starting from taxation, without grounding it in the relationship between taxation and its use for the fulfilment of social rights.

The recent experience of the GMT serves as a revealing case study: without a social and global contract aimed at eradicating tax competition, such initiatives risk producing unintended outcomes. In particular, the GMT framework may not result in the taxation of all profits, but only of those considered in excess of a normal return—defined as a percentage of the value of tangible assets and payroll reported in a given jurisdiction.[119] As highlighted by recent studies,[120] the intuitive expectation that a Global Minimum Tax (GMT) will necessarily lead to higher corporate tax revenues must be approached with caution. It is also worth noting that the potential impact of the GMT on existing statutory corporate tax rates remains uncertain, as much will depend on the strategic responses of both countries and multinational corporations. Moreover, the GMT is a binding agreement without enforceable sanctions in the event of non-compliance—an issue that underscores the necessity of associating supranational taxation with a supranational authority capable of ensuring its implementation.

The narrow focus of much of the literature is on how the GMT may influence tax competition. While this is appropriate to the extent that it seeks to address the harmful race to the bottom in international tax policy that has evolved over decades, it is also limited. That perspective remains overly focused on curbing the opportunistic behaviour of multinationals, rather than addressing the deeper institutional changes that would be necessary to modify such behaviour in the first place. From this standpoint, it becomes clear why the Rawlsian framework places greater emphasis on the creation of just institutions rather than merely on taxation, as only just institutions can convert opportunistic competition into a true social contract.

The GMT is indeed a significant step toward limiting economic power. However, it should also serve as a reminder that tax competition has been one of the key drivers of growing inequality in recent decades. Therefore, taxing without transforming the foundational principles of both the tax system and prevailing economic behaviours risks becoming little more than a symbolic gesture. In DWS, such challenges can only be addressed within the broader context of a global social contract. An insightful development in this direction is the recent proposal for global constitutionalism.[121] This framework aims to address the asymmetry between the global reach of economic power and the national scope of political constitutions. Importantly, the proposal seeks to establish just institutions—in the Rawlsian sense—to safeguard social rights and ensure equal opportunities.[122]

[119] Hugger et al. (2024).

[120] Haufler and Kato (2024); Hebous and Keen (2023); Janeba and Schjelderup (2023); Johannesen (2022).

[121] Ferrajoli (2022).

[122] On this point, see Kukathas and Pettit (1995).

In a global political context where power is increasingly plural and distributed across various entities—including non-state actors and corporations—decisions made by the few can dramatically shape the economic and social conditions of the many. This situation implies that the actions of a small, unelected elite may impose substantial social opportunity costs on people who are excluded from the decision-making process. Such dynamics represent a profound erosion of the democratic principle of political equality. Attempts have been made to reconcile these asymmetries through the concept of stakeholder democracy, which seeks to include all those affected by a given political decision—regardless of formal political membership—on the basis of the affectedness principle.[123] However, this principle does not constitute a true solution, as it is not equivalent to a common scheme of political institutions based on membership. Rather, it serves as an implicit acknowledgment of the weakening of democratic processes when observed from a global perspective.

References

Avi-Yonah, R. S. (2002). Why tax the rich? Efficiency, equity, and progressive taxation. *The Yale Law Journal, 111*, 1391–1416.

Baker, D. (2006). *The conservative Nanny State: How the wealthy use the state to stay rich and get richer.* Center for Economic and Policy Research.

Barnes, L. (2015). Public opinion, predistribution and progressive taxation. In P. Diamond, C. Chwalisz (Eds.), *The predistribution agenda: Tackling inequality and supporting sustainable growth* (Part I - chapter 1, pp. 33–48). I.B. Tauris.

Blum, W. J., & Kalven, H. J. (1953). *The uneasy case for progressive taxation.* University of Chicago Press.

Brennan, G., & Buchanan, J. M. (1980). *The power to tax: Analytical foundations of a fiscal constitutions.* Cambridge University Press.

Buchanan, J. M. (1976). Taxation in fiscal exchange. *Journal of Public Economics, 6*, 17–29.

Busemeyer, M. R. (2015). Social investments, skills and inequality - the importance of institutional design. In C. Chwalisz, P. Diamond (Eds.), *The predistribution agenda - tackling inequality and supporting sustainable growth* (chapter 10). I.B. Tauris.

Carnazza, G., Liberati, P., & Resce, G. (2023). Income-related unmet needs in the European countries. *Socio-Economic Planning Sciences, 87*(A), 101542.

[123] Macdonald (2012).

Castles, F., & Mitchell, D. (1992). Identifying welfare state regimes: The links between politics, instruments and outcomes. *Governance, 5*(1), 1–26.

Clark, B., & Gintis, H. (1978). Rawlsian justice and economic systems. *Philosophy and Public Affairs, 7*(4), 302–325.

Diamond, L. (2015). Facing up to the democratic recession. *Journal of Democracy, 26*(1), 141–155.

Edmundson, W. A. (2017). *John Rawls: Reticent socialist.* University Printing House.

Elkins, D. (2019). Consumption taxation in Rawls' theory of justice. *Cornell Journal of Law and Public Policy, 29*(4), 799–860.

Esping-Andersen, G. (1990). *The three worlds of welfare capitalism.* Polity Press.

Ezrow, L., & Krause, W. (2023). Voter turnout decline and party responsiveness. *British Journal of Political Science, 53*, 85–103.

Fernandez Manzano, J. A. (2022). Democratic equality and Rawls's criticism of welfare state capitalism. *Ethics, Politics and Society, 5*(2), 80–95.

Ferrajoli, L. (2022). *Per una Costituzione della terra - L'umanità del bivio.* Feltrinelli.

Fishkin, J. (2014), *Bottlenecks: A new theory of equal opportunity.* Oxford University Press.

Fitoussi, J. (2004). *La Démocratie et le Marché.* Grasset et Fasquelle.

Fitzpatrick, S. (1998). Homelessness in the European Union. In M. Kleinman, M. Stephens, W. Mattzenetter (Eds.), *European integration and housing policy.* Routledge.

Flecker, J. (2010). Fragmenting labour: organisational restructuring, employment relations and the dynamics of national regulatory frameworks. *Work Organisation, Labour and Globalisation, 4*(1), 8–23.

Forrester, K. (2019). The New egalitarians. In K. Forrester (Ed.), *In the shadow of justice - Postwar liberalism and the remaking of political philosophy* (chapter 4). Princeton University Press.

Freeman, S. (2007). *Rawls.* Routledge.

Freeman, S. (2018). *Liberalism and distributive justice.* Oxford University Press.

Fried, B. H. (2003). Proportionate taxation as a fair division of the social surplus: The strange career of an idea. *Economics and Philosophy, 19*(2), 211–239.

Gamble, A. (2015). Welfare states after the crisis. In C. Chwalisz, P. Diamond (Eds.), *The predistribution agenda - Tackling inequality and supporting sustainable growth* (Introductions; pp. 23–30). I.B. Tauris.

Gilens, M. (2005). Inequality and democratic responsiveness. *The Public Opinion Quarterly, 69*(5), 778–796.

Graetz, M. J. (1997). *The decline (and fall?) of the income tax.* W.W. Norton and Company.

Gregg, P. (2015). The potential and limits of predistribution in the UK - Tackling inequality and poverty. In P. Diamond, C. Chwalisz (Eds.), *The predistribution agenda: Tackling inequality and supporting sustainable growth* (chapter 4). I.B. Tauris.

Groves, R., Murie, A., & Watson, C. (2007). Four worlds of welfare and housing. In R. Groves, A. Murie, C. Watson (Eds.), *Housing and the new welfare state: Perspectives from East Asia and Europe* (chapter 1). Aldershot.

Hacker, J. S. (2011). The institutional foundations of middle-class democracy. *Policy Network*, 33–37.

Hacker, J. S. (2015). The premise of predistribution. In C. Chwalisz, P. Diamond (Eds.), *The predistribution agenda - Tackling inequality and supporting sustainable growth* (Foreword). I.B. Tauris.

Haig, R. M. (1921). *The concept of income - Economic and legal aspects in the federal income tax* (pp. 1–28). Columbia University Press.

Hanushek, E. A., & Woessmann, L. (2012). Do better schools lead to more growth? cognitive skills, economic outcomes, and causation. *Journal of Economic Growth, 17*, 267–321.

Harloe, M. (1995). *The people's home: Social rented housing in Europe and America.* Blackwell.

Haufler, A., & Kato, H. (2024). *A global minimum tax for large firms only: Implications for tax competition.* CESifo working papers No. 11087.

Hebous, S., & Keen, M. (2023). Pareto-improving minimum corporate taxation. *Journal of Public Economics, 225*, 104952.

Heckman, J., Pinto, R., & Savelyev, P. (2013). Understanding the mechanisms through which an influential early childhood program boosted adult outcomes. *American Economic Review, 103*(6), 2052–2086.

Hettich, W., & Winer, S. L. (1999). *Democratic choice and taxation - A theoretical and empirical analysis.* Cambridge University Press.

Hirschman, A. O. (1990). *I Tre Continenti.* Giulio Einaudi.

Huber, E., & Stephens, J. D. (2015). Predistribution and redistribution - Alternative or complementary policies? In C. Chwalisz, P. Diamond (Eds.), *The predistribution agenda - Tackling inequality and supporting sustainable growth* (chapter 3). I.B. Tauris.

Hugger, F., Gonzalez Cabral, A. C., Bucci, M., Gesualdo, M., & O'Reilly, P. (2024). *The global minimum tax and the taxation of MNE profits.* OECD Taxation Working Papers no. 68, Paris.

Janeba, E., & Schjelderup, G. (2023). The global minimum tax raises more revenues than you think, or much less. *Journal of International Economics, 145*, 103837.

Johannesen, N. (2022). The global minimum tax. *Journal of Public Economics, 212*, 104709.

Kaldor, N. (1955). *An expenditure tax.* George Allen and Unwin.

Kiefer, D., & Rada, C. (2015). Profit maximising goes global: the race to the bottom. *Cambridge Journal of Economics, 39*(5), 1333–1350.

Krouse, R., & McPherson, M. (1988). Capitalism, "Property-Owning Democracy", and the Welfare State. In A. Gutmann (Ed.), *Democracy and the welfare state* (chapter 4). Princeton University Press.

Kukathas, C., & Pettit, P. (1995). *Rawls - A theory of justice and its critics.* Polity Press.

Lowe, R., & Jones, M. (2002). *From Beveridge to Blair - The first fifty years of Britain's welfare state 1948–98.* Manchester University Press.

Macdonald, T. (2012). Citizens or stakeholders? Exclusion, equality and legitimacy in global stakeholder democracy. In D. Archibugi, M. Koenig-Archibugi, R. Marchetti (Eds.), *Global democracy: Normative and empirical perspectives* (pp. 47–67). Cambridge University Press.

Marshall, A. [1920] (1947). *Principles of economics - An introductory volume* (Eighth Edition (reprinted)). Macmilland and Co.

Marshall, T. H. (1965). *Social policy.* Hutchinson.

Meade, J. E. (1964). *Efficiency, equality and the ownership of property.* George Allen and Unwin.

Michelman, F. I. (2003). Rawls on constitutionalism and constitutional law. In S. Freeman (Ed.), *The Cambridge companion to Rawls* (pp. 394–425). Cambridge University Press.

Nickell, S. (2004). Poverty and Worklessness in Britain. *The Economic Journal, 114*(494), C1–C25.

O'Neill, M. (2020). Power, predistribution, and social justice. *Philosophy, 95*, 63–91.

O'Neill, M., & Williamson, T. (2012). *Property-owning democracy: Rawls and beyond.* Wiley-Blackwell.

Offe, C. (1987). Democracy against the welfare state? Structural foundations of neoconservative political opportunities. *Political Theory, 15*(4), 501–537.

Petroni, L. (2015). John Rawls and the social maximum. *Revista Diacritica, 29*(2), 65–86.

Piketty, T., Saez, E., & Stantcheva, S. (2014). Optimal taxation of top labor incomes: A tale of three elasticities. *American Economic Journal: Economic Policy, 6*(1), 230–271.

Quigley, J., & Raphael, S. (2001). The economics of homelessness: the evidence from North America. *European Journal of Housing Policy, 1*(3), 323–336.

Rawls, J. (1999). *A theory of justice: Revised edition.* Harvard University Press.

Rawls, J. (2001). *Justice as fairness: A restatement.* Harvard University Press.

Rawls, J. (2008). *Lectures on the history of political philosophy.* Belknap, Harvard University Press.

Roemer, J. E. (1994). *A Future for socialism.* Harvard University Press.

Romer, P. (1990). Endogenous technological change. *Journal of Political Economy, 99*(5), S71–S102.

Rossi, E. (1946). *Abolire la miseria.* La Fiaccola.

Rothstein, B. (1998). *Just institutions matter - The moral and political logic of the universal welfare state.* Cambridge University Press.

Saez, E., & Zucman, G. (2019). *The triumph of injustice - How the rich dodge taxes and how to make them pay.* W.W. Norton and Company.

Scanlon, T. M. (2018). *Why does inequality matter?* Oxford University Press.

Schanz, G. (1896). Der einkommensbegriff und die einkommensteuergesetze. *FinanzArchiv, 13*, 1–87

Schefczyk, M. (2013). Background justice over time: Property-owning democracy vs. a realistically utopian welfare state. *Analyse and Kritik, 2*, 1–20.

Simons, H. C. (1938). *Personal income taxation - The definition of income as a problem of fiscal policy.* University of Chicago Press.

Slobodian, Q. (2023). *Crack-up capitalism. Market radicals and the dream of a world without democracy.* MacMillan, Penguin Random House.

Stephens, M., & Fitzpatrick, S. (2007). Welfare regimes, housing systems and homelessness: How are they linked? *European Journal of Homelessness, 1*, 201–212.

Streeck, W. (2016). How will capitalism end? *New Left Review, 87*, 35–64.

Swank, D. (2002). *Global capital, political institutions, and policy change in developed welfare states.* Cambridge University Press.

Thiel, P. (2009). The education of a libertarian. *Cato Unbound.* https://www.catounbound.org/2009/04/13/peter-thiel/education-libertarian/.

Thomas, A. (2016). *Republic of equals: Predistribution and property-owning democracy.* Oxford University Press.

Torgersen, U. (1987). Housing: the wobbly pillar under the welfare state. *Scandinavian Housing and Planning Research, 4*(supl), 116–126.

Tsarouhas, D. (2015). Predistribution and labour market actors - Looking at the trade union movement. In C. Chwalisz, P. Diamond (eds.), *The predistribution agenda - Tackling inequality and supporting sustainable growth* (chapter 9). I.B. Tauris.

Wade, R. (2013). How high inequality plus neoliberal governance weakens democracy. *Challenge, 56*(6), 5–37.

Walraevens, B. (2023). Rawls's maximin and optimal taxation theory. *The European Journal of the History of Economic Thought, 30*(5), 860–882.

Watson, D. (2009). Welfare rights and human rights. *Journal of Social Policy, 6*(1), 31–46.

Weale, A. (2013). The property-owning democracy versus the welfare state. *Analyse and Kritik, 1*, 37–54.

West, A. (2007). Poverty and educational achievement: why do children from low-income families tend to do less well at school? *Journal of Poverty and Social Justice, 15*(3), 283–297.
Williamson, T. (2013). Constitutionalizing property-owning democracy. *The Good Society, 22*(1), 74–90.
Wolf, M. (2023). *The crisis of democratic capitalism*. Penguin Press.
Wolff, R. P. (1977). *Understanding Rawls: A reconstruction and critique of "A Theory of Justice"*. Princeton University Press.

Author Index

Note: Page numbers followed by 'n' refer to notes.

P. Liberati, M. Paradiso, *Rebuilding Fiscal Democracy*,
https://doi.org/10.1057/978-3-032-04859-2

Subject Index

Note: Page numbers followed by 'n' refer to notes.

P. Liberati, M. Paradiso, *Rebuilding Fiscal Democracy*,
https://doi.org/10.1057/978-3-032-04859-2

FSC
www.fsc.org
MIX
Papier | Fördert gute Waldnutzung
FSC® C083411

Kolibri 360 GmbH
Ferdinand-Jühlke-Straße 7
99095 Erfurt, Deutschland
produktsicherheit@kolibri360.de